CST-11 NEW YORK STATE TEACHER CERTIFICATION SERIES

This is your
PASSBOOK for...

English to Speakers of Other Languages

Test Preparation Study Guide
Questions & Answers

COPYRIGHT NOTICE

This book is SOLELY intended for, is sold ONLY to, and its use is RESTRICTED to individual, bona fide applicants or candidates who qualify by virtue of having seriously filed applications for appropriate license, certificate, professional and/or promotional advancement, higher school matriculation, scholarship, or other legitimate requirements of education and/or governmental authorities.

This book is NOT intended for use, class instruction, tutoring, training, duplication, copying, reprinting, excerption, or adaptation, etc., by:

1) Other publishers
2) Proprietors and/or Instructors of "Coaching" and/or Preparatory Courses
3) Personnel and/or Training Divisions of commercial, industrial, and governmental organizations
4) Schools, colleges, or universities and/or their departments and staffs, including teachers and other personnel
5) Testing Agencies or Bureaus
6) Study groups which seek by the purchase of a single volume to copy and/or duplicate and/or adapt this material for use by the group as a whole without having purchased individual volumes for each of the members of the group
7) Et al.

Such persons would be in violation of appropriate Federal and State statutes.

PROVISION OF LICENSING AGREEMENTS – Recognized educational, commercial, industrial, and governmental institutions and organizations, and others legitimately engaged in educational pursuits, including training, testing, and measurement activities, may address request for a licensing agreement to the copyright owners, who will determine whether, and under what conditions, including fees and charges, the materials in this book may be used them. In other words, a licensing facility exists for the legitimate use of the material in this book on other than an individual basis. However, it is asseverated and affirmed here that the material in this book CANNOT be used without the receipt of the express permission of such a licensing agreement from the Publishers. Inquiries re licensing should be addressed to the company, attention rights and permissions department.

All rights reserved, including the right of reproduction in whole or in part, in any form or by any means, electronic or mechanical, including photocopying, recording, or by any information storage and retrieval system, without permission in writing from the Publisher.

Copyright © 2025 by
National Learning Corporation

212 Michael Drive, Syosset, NY 11791
(516) 921-8888 • www.passbooks.com
E-mail: info@passbooks.com

PASSBOOK® SERIES

THE *PASSBOOK® SERIES* has been created to prepare applicants and candidates for the ultimate academic battlefield – the examination room.

At some time in our lives, each and every one of us may be required to take an examination – for validation, matriculation, admission, qualification, registration, certification, or licensure.

Based on the assumption that every applicant or candidate has met the basic formal educational standards, has taken the required number of courses, and read the necessary texts, the *PASSBOOK® SERIES* furnishes the one special preparation which may assure passing with confidence, instead of failing with insecurity. Examination questions – together with answers – are furnished as the basic vehicle for study so that the mysteries of the examination and its compounding difficulties may be eliminated or diminished by a sure method.

This book is meant to help you pass your examination provided that you qualify and are serious in your objective.

The entire field is reviewed through the huge store of content information which is succinctly presented through a provocative and challenging approach – the question-and-answer method.

A climate of success is established by furnishing the correct answers at the end of each test.

You soon learn to recognize types of questions, forms of questions, and patterns of questioning. You may even begin to anticipate expected outcomes.

You perceive that many questions are repeated or adapted so that you can gain acute insights, which may enable you to score many sure points.

You learn how to confront new questions, or types of questions, and to attack them confidently and work out the correct answers.

You note objectives and emphases, and recognize pitfalls and dangers, so that you may make positive educational adjustments.

Moreover, you are kept fully informed in relation to new concepts, methods, practices, and directions in the field.

You discover that you are actually taking the examination all the time: you are preparing for the examination by "taking" an examination, not by reading extraneous and/or supererogatory textbooks.

In short, this PASSBOOK®, used directedly, should be an important factor in helping you to pass your test.

NEW YORK STATE TEACHER CERTIFICATION EXAMINATIONS™
INTRODUCTION

GENERAL INFORMATION

About the Testing Program

Those seeking a New York State teaching certificate for the common branch subjects in prekindergarten through grade 6 or for academic subjects in the secondary grades 7 through 12, i.e., English, a language other than English, mathematics, a science (biology, chemistry, earth science, physics), or social studies, must pass the New York State Teacher Certification Examinations (NYSTCE®) as part of the requirements for certification.

Those seeking a New York State teaching certificate in other areas may need to achieve qualifying scores on the NYSTCE® as indicated in the table which follows.

The New York State Teacher Certification Examinations™ program consists of the

- Liberal Arts and Sciences Test (LAST)
- Elementary and Secondary Assessment of Teaching Skills Written (ATS-W)
- Content Specialty Tests (CSTs)
- Language Proficiency Assessments (LPAs)
- Assessment of Teaching Skills - Performance (ATS-P) (Video)

These exams provide an objective basis of competency and skill for teaching in New York State.

For the requirements, check the summary table of testing requirements which follows.

Test Development

The New York State Teacher Certification Examinations™ are criterion referenced and objective based. A criterion-referenced test is designed to measure a candidate's knowledge and skills in relation to an established standard rather than in relation to the performance of other candidates. The purpose of these exams is to certify candidates who have demonstrated requisite knowledge and skills necessary for a public school teacher.

> The New York State Teacher Certification Examination C"NYSTCE.") program was developed and is administered by the New York State Education Department ("NYSED® ") and National Evaluation Systems, Inc. ("NES"), and this test preparation guide was neither developed in connection with these organizations, nor is it endorsed by them. The NES® and NYSTCE® names and logos are registered service marks of. National Evaluation Systems, Inc. for use with testing services and related products.

An individual's performance on a test is evaluated against an established standard. The passing score for each test is established by the New York State Commissioner of Education based on the professional judgments and recommendations of New York State educators. Examinees who do not pass a test may retake it at any of the subsequent scheduled test administrations.

Description of the Tests

The following is a description of the tests within the NYSTCE® program.

Liberal Arts and Sciences Test (LAST). The Liberal Arts and Sciences Test consists of multiple-choice test questions and a written assignment. Candidates are asked to demonstrate conceptual and analytical skills, critical-thinking and communication skills, and multicultural awareness. The test covers scientific and mathematical processes, historical and social scientific awareness, artistic expression and the humanities, communication skills, and written n analysis and expression. The Liberal Arts and Sciences Test is required for a provisional certificate.

Elementary and Secondary Versions of the Assessment of Teaching Skills - Written (ATS-W). There are two versions of the Assessment of Teaching Skills - Written (ATS-W). The elementary ATS-W should be taken by individuals seeking a PreK-6, common branch subject teaching certificate. The secondary ATS-W should be taken by individuals seeking a certificate for a secondary academic subject. Individuals seeking a certificate in other titles may take either the elementary or the secondary ATS-W. The ATS-W is required for a provisional certificate.

The elementary and secondary versions of the Assessment of Teaching Skills - Written consists of multiple-choice test questions and a written assignment. These tests address knowledge of the learner, instructional planning and assessment, instructional delivery, and the professional environment.

Content Specialty Tests (CSTs). There are currently 21 Content Specialty Tests. For a complete list of test titles, see the list that follows.

The Content Specialty Tests (except Japanese, Russian, Mandarin, Cantonese, Hebrew, and Greek) contain multiple-choice test questions. The CSTs for languages other than English also include audiotaped listening and speaking components and writing components. The CSTs are required for a permanent certificate.

Language Proficiency Assessments (ELPA-C, ELPA-N, TLPAs). The Language Proficiency Assessments are required for ESOL certificates and for bilingual education extension certificates in New York State.

Assessment of Teaching Skills - Performance (ATS-P) (video). The Assessment of Teaching Skills - Performance (ATS-P) (video) is one requirement for individuals seeking a permanent New York State teaching certificate in specified areas. For this assessment, candidates are required to prepare a videotape of their instruction with students who are part of their regular teaching assignments in grades PreK through 12. The teaching skills assessed by the ATS-P (video) are defined by the five objectives in the Instructional Delivery subarea of the Assessment of Teaching Skills test framework.

From the official announcement for instructional purposes

TESTS

Test (Test Code)

Liberal Arts and Sciences Test (LAST) (01)
Elementary Assessment of Teaching Skills - Written (ATS-W) (90)
Secondary Assessment of Teaching Skills - Written (ATS-W) (91)
Elementary Education (02)
English (03)
Mathematics (04)
Social Studies (05)
Biology (06)
Chemistry (07)
Earth Science (08)
Physics (09)
Early Childhood (21)
Latin (10)
Cantonese (11)
French (12)
German (13)
Greek (14)
Hebrew (15)
Italian (16)
Japanese (17)
Mandarin (18)
Russian (19)
Spanish (20)
English to Speakers of Other Languages (ESOL) (22)
English Language Proficiency Assessment for Classroom Personnel (ELPA-C) (23)
English Language Proficiency Assessment for Nonclassroom Personnel (ELPA-N) (25)
Target Language Proficiency Assessment - Spanish (24)
Target Language Proficiency Assessment other than Spanish

NEW YORK STATE TEACHER CERTIFICATION TESTING REQUIREMENTS

(Commissioner's Regulation) Teaching Certificates	Current Requirements	Projected Requirements
(8 NYCRR 80.15) PreK-6, Common Branch Subjects	LAST — Provisional ATS-W — Provisional CST (Elementary Education) — Permanent ATS-P — Permanent	
7-9 Extension	Same as base certificate, PLUS: CST in academic subject — Permanent	Same as current requirements
Early Childhood Annotation (PreK-3)	CST in annotation — Permanent	
(8 NYCRR 80.16) 7-12 Academic Subjects, e.g., English, Language other than English, Mathematics, Science (Biology, Chemistry, Earth Science, Physics), Social Studies	LAST — Provisional ATS-W — Provisional CST (in academic subject) — Permanent ATS-P — Permanent	Same as current requirements
5-6 Extension	Same as base certificate	
(8 NYCRR 80.9) Bilingual Education [Extension]	Same as base certificate, PLUS: LPA in English (oral)* — Prov./Perm. LPA in Target Language (oral & written)* — Prov./Perm.	Same as current requirements
(8 NYCRR 80.10) English to speakers of other languages (ESOL)	LAST* — Provisional ATS-W* — Provisional LPA in English (oral)* — Provisional CST* (ESOL) — Permanent ATS-P* — Permanent	Same as current requirements
(8 NYCRR 80.5) Occupational Subjects, e.g. Agricultural Subjects, Business/Distributive Education, Health Occupations, Trade Subjects, Technical Subjects, Home Economics Subjects	Baccalaureate-based certificates: LAST + ATS-W or NTE Core Battery — Provisional Associate & non-degree-based certificate titles: ATS-W or NTE Core Battery — Permanent	Baccalaureate-based certificates: LAST — Provisional ATS-W — Provisional CST — Permanent ATS-P — Permanent Associate & non-degree-based certificate titles: ATS-W — Provisional ATS-P — Permanent

NEW YORK STATE TEACHER CERTIFICATION TESTING REQUIREMENTS

(Commissioner's Regulation) Teaching Certificates	Current Requirements	Projected Requirements
(8 NYCRR 80.6) <u>Special Education</u>, e.g. Special Education, Blind/ Partially Sighted, Deaf/ Hearing Impaired <hr> Speech/Hearing Handicapped	LAST & ATS-W or NTE Core Battery — Provisional	Same as for PreK-6 or 7-12 certificate, PLUS: Special Education Supplement to ATS-W — Provisional Special Education supplement to ATS-P — Permanent
(8 NYCRR 80.7) Reading	LAST & ATS-W or NTE Core Battery — Provisional	Same as for PreK-6 or 7-12 certificate, PLUS: CST in Reading — Permanent
(8 NYCRR 80.8) School Media Specialist	LAST + ATS-W or NTE Core Battery — Provisional	LAST — Provisional ATS-W — Provisional CST — Permanent ATS-P — Permanent
(8 NYCRR 80.17) <u>Special Subjects</u>, e.g. Art, Business/Distributive Education, Dance, Health, Home Economics, Music, Physical Education, Recreation, Speech, Technology Education	LAST + ATS-W or NTE Core Battery — Provisional	LAST — Provisional ATS-W — Provisional CST — Permanent ATS-P — Permanent

LAST = Liberal Arts & Sciences Test
ATS-W = Assessment of Teaching Skills - Written
CST = Content Specialty Test
ATS-P = Assessment of Teaching Skills - Performance (video)
LPA = Language Proficiency Assessment

FOR FURTHER INFORMATION

If you have questions regarding which test(s) you must take, contact the teacher certification contact person at your college or:

NEW YORK STATE EDUCATION DEPARTMENT
OFFICE OF TEACHING
CULTURAL EDUCATION CENTER
ALBANY, N.Y. 12230

TELEPHONE: (518) 474-3901
9:00-11:45 A.M., 12:45-4:30 P.M. Eastern Time

Relay center telephone number for the deaf within New York State: 1-800-622-1220

Nationwide AT&T Relay Operator for the Deaf: 1-800-855-2880 (TTY)

If you have questions regarding the Test Registration, Administration Procedures, Admission Ticket, or Score Report, contact:

NYSTCE
NATIONAL EVALUATION SYSTEMS, INC.
30 GATEHOUSE ROAD
P.O. BOX 660
AMHERST, MA 01004-9008

TELEPHONE: (413) 256-2882
9:00 A.M. - 5:00 P.M. Eastern Time

Telephone number for the deaf: (413) 256-8032 (TTY)

NEW YORK STATE TEACHER CERTIFICATION EXAMINATIONS™

FIELD 22: ENGLISH TO SPEAKERS OF OTHER LANGUAGES TEST FRAMEWORK

Foundations of ESOL Instruction
Developing English Language Proficiency Across the Curriculum
The ESOL Program
Developing English Language Proficiency Across the Curriculum:
Constructed-Response Assignment

The New York State teacher of English to speakers of other languages (ESOL) has the knowledge and skills to teach effectively in New York State public schools. The ESOL teacher understands the ways in which students acquire first and subsequent languages and is able to provide developmentally appropriate learning experiences to support English-language development. The ESOL teacher understands that many factors—culture, socioeconomic status, prior learning—influence an English language learner's development of English. The ESOL teacher is able to use a variety of methods and techniques to develop and assess the listening, speaking, reading, and writing proficiency of English language learners. The ESOL teacher recognizes that there are several different models of ESOL instruction and that adaptations must be made to design instruction that addresses the specific strengths and needs of each student. The ESOL teacher collaborates with other teachers to help students develop cognitive-academic language skills and content-area knowledge. The ESOL teacher understands that the English language learner is a student who communicates both in the school environment and in the community. The ESOL teacher demonstrates sensitivity to and respect for students who are in various stages of first- and subsequent-language acquisition, and provides students with opportunities for authentic, purposeful, and meaningful interactions with the English language.

FIELD 22: ENGLISH TO SPEAKERS OF OTHER LANGUAGES
TEST FRAMEWORK

SUBAREA I—FOUNDATIONS OF ESOL INSTRUCTION

0001 Understand basic linguistic concepts and their application to ESOL instruction.

For example:

- applying knowledge of phonetics and phonology (e.g., distinguishing among classes of sound)
- applying knowledge of English morphology and lexicon to analyze a word's structure, function, and meaning
- identifying syntactic features (e.g., a verb phrase) in sentence context
- identifying discourse features (e.g., cohesion) in a textual context
- applying knowledge of linguistic concepts in interlanguage analysis
- applying knowledge of the structure of the English language

0002 Understand basic sociolinguistic concepts related to ESOL instruction.

For example:

- demonstrating knowledge of sociolinguistic concepts (e.g., dialect diversity in English, intercultural differences in communication styles, codeswitching)
- demonstrating knowledge of academic discourses
- demonstrating knowledge of language variation
- demonstrating knowledge of the appropriate roles of written and spoken Standard English

0003 Understand the process of language acquisition.

For example:

- analyzing major theories of first- and second-language acquisition
- demonstrating knowledge of stages and sequences in second-language acquisition in terms of the learners' individual characteristics
- demonstrating knowledge of the learning processes (e.g., metacognitive and cognitive strategies) that are involved in internalizing language rules for second-language acquisition
- applying knowledge of the role of the first language in second-language acquisition and learning (e.g., language transfer, interlanguage development)

FIELD 22: ENGLISH TO SPEAKERS OF OTHER LANGUAGES
TEST FRAMEWORK

0004 Understand instructional approaches, methods, and techniques in second-language acquisition and learning.

    For example:

- analyzing the theoretical bases of historical and current instructional approaches (e.g., communicative language teaching, functional-notional approach, content-based language instruction, theme-based language instruction)

- applying strategies for integrating assessment with second-language instruction

- selecting classroom activities to accommodate the diverse needs of learners and instructional methods

- choosing appropriate instructional practices to achieve curricular objectives

- demonstrating knowledge of classroom organization strategies to create opportunities for meaningful communication

0005 Understand factors that may influence English language learners' development of English.

    For example:

- analyzing cultural and environmental factors that may affect students' English language development (e.g., age, motivation)

- analyzing social and psychological factors that may affect students' English language development (e.g., personality, cultural transition)

- demonstrating knowledge of nonlinguistic and sociocultural aspects of English that are challenging for English language learners (e.g., idioms, nonverbal elements, turn-taking features)

- demonstrating knowledge of the ways in which educational background may affect literacy development

FIELD 22: ENGLISH TO SPEAKERS OF OTHER LANGUAGES
TEST FRAMEWORK

0006 Understand methods and techniques for assessing students' progress in developing English communication skills.

For example:

- demonstrating knowledge of different types of assessments (e.g., norm- and criterion-referenced, standardized, informal) and important concepts used in evaluating the usefulness and appropriateness of an assessment (e.g., reliability, validity, practicality)

- analyzing formal and informal methods of assessing specific dimensions of language proficiency

- demonstrating knowledge of informal assessment strategies and approaches (e.g., observational checklists)

- demonstrating an understanding of sources and causes of potential bias in assessment

SUBAREA II—DEVELOPING ENGLISH LANGUAGE PROFICIENCY ACROSS THE CURRICULUM

0007 Understand methods and techniques for developing and assessing the listening proficiency of English language learners.

For example:

- analyzing the role of prior knowledge in aural comprehension

- demonstrating knowledge of listening skills required in different situations (e.g., listening for gist vs. listening for details, listening to a lecture vs. listening to the context of a conversation)

- selecting appropriate classroom listening activities to achieve given instructional purposes

- selecting appropriate classroom listening activities that build on and expand students' real-life situations and experiences

- selecting or creating appropriate assessments for given testing purposes and situations

FIELD 22: ENGLISH TO SPEAKERS OF OTHER LANGUAGES
TEST FRAMEWORK

0008 **Understand methods and techniques for developing and assessing the speaking skills of English language learners.**

For example:

- accommodating and identifying the instructional needs of students at various levels of oral proficiency
- selecting appropriate classroom speaking activities (e.g., paired and small-group conversations, choral speaking, creative drama, role playing) to meet varied instructional purposes
- selecting appropriate classroom strategies to extend students' communicative competence and social interaction skills
- applying knowledge of the role of oral language in literacy development
- selecting or creating appropriate assessments for given testing purposes and situations

0009 **Understand methods and techniques for developing and assessing the reading proficiency of English language learners, for the dual purposes of learning to read and reading to learn.**

For example:

- demonstrating knowledge of principles of effective reading instruction
- demonstrating knowledge of the transferability of first-language literacy skills into English
- identifying strategies that help English language learners utilize their spoken English to develop their reading proficiency in English (e.g., language experience approach)
- demonstrating knowledge of the interrelationship between decoding and comprehension in English
- applying knowledge of schema theory in reading instruction
- applying knowledge of various literary genres and purposes for reading
- selecting and adapting appropriate classroom activities for given instructional purposes and for English language learners at different literacy levels and English language proficiency levels
- selecting or creating appropriate assessments for given testing purposes and situations

FIELD 22: ENGLISH TO SPEAKERS OF OTHER LANGUAGES
TEST FRAMEWORK

0010 Understand methods and techniques for developing and assessing the writing skills of English language learners.

For example:

- analyzing the role of other communicative modes (e.g., speaking, reading) in developing the writing skills of English language learners
- applying knowledge of the writing process in designing activities to develop students' writing proficiency
- identifying strategies for developing students' organization in writing and their ability to write in different academic genres (e.g., narration, analysis)
- selecting purposeful writing activities that are appropriate to a range of ages and proficiency levels (e.g., friendly letters, book reports, research papers)
- applying instructional strategies that address conventions of English grammar, usage, and mechanics
- selecting or creating appropriate assessments for given testing purposes and situations

0011 Understand the selection, adaptation, and use of materials for various instructional purposes in the ESOL classroom.

For example:

- defining appropriate criteria for evaluating instructional materials
- selecting appropriate materials for given instructional purposes (e.g., making content accessible)
- demonstrating knowledge of the uses of content-area texts, children's and adolescent literature, and multicultural literature in the ESOL classroom
- creating and adapting materials to meet the needs, interests, and proficiency levels of students
- recognizing ways to integrate technologies in the classroom for given instructional purposes

FIELD 22: ENGLISH TO SPEAKERS OF OTHER LANGUAGES
TEST FRAMEWORK

0012 Understand approaches to facilitating content-area learning for English language learners.

For example:

- demonstrating knowledge of techniques for using students' linguistic and cultural diversity to enhance content-area learning

- identifying linguistic characteristics and applying methods for developing students' cognitive-academic language proficiency in content areas

- demonstrate the ability to devise and implement thematic units that integrate content and language objectives and help English language learners acquire content-area knowledge and skills

- utilizing strategies for selecting and adapting content-area curricula to meet the cognitive and linguistic needs of English language learners

- applying knowledge of instructional strategies that help students build on their prior knowledge and experience

- analyzing the benefits of collaboration between the ESOL teacher and content-area teachers

SUBAREA III—THE ESOL PROGRAM

0013 Understand historical, legal, and administrative aspects of programs serving English language learners.

For example:

- demonstrating knowledge of historical and current issues related to ESOL instruction

- applying the provisions of federal and state laws and regulations governing the delivery of ESOL instruction

- analyzing knowledge of the roles and responsibilities of teachers, parents, and others in the education of English language learners

- demonstrating understanding of the relationship between the ESOL program and other school programs

- demonstrating awareness of New York State Learning Standards for English as a Second Language

FIELD 22: ENGLISH TO SPEAKERS OF OTHER LANGUAGES
TEST FRAMEWORK

0014 Understand approaches to instruction that are appropriate to the diversity of the English language learner population and that meet various student needs.

For example:

- recognizing cross-cultural and linguistic differences in communication styles (e.g., rhetorical styles, conversational styles)
- demonstrating knowledge of ways to acknowledge and affirm various types of diversity in the ESOL classroom, the school, and the community
- applying knowledge of assessments to determine whether students' needs are based on language differences and/or language disorders
- making appropriate instructional adaptations for English language learners with special educational needs (e.g., learning disabilities, giftedness) and for learners whose previous formal academic instruction has been severely interrupted
- selecting and applying instructional strategies appropriate to students' varied learning styles

0015 Understand the planning and management of ESOL instruction in a variety of settings.

For example:

- demonstrating an understanding of different settings/models of ESOL instruction (e.g., sheltered instruction, integrated programs) and management strategies appropriate to each
- selecting appropriate ways to organize instruction for students at different ages, stages of cognitive development, and proficiency levels
- analyzing the advantages of various physical arrangements in adapting a classroom for ESOL instruction
- selecting appropriate ways of grouping students for instructional purposes

FIELD 22: ENGLISH TO SPEAKERS OF OTHER LANGUAGES
TEST FRAMEWORK

0016 Understand methods of relating ESOL instruction to students' lives outside the classroom.

For example:

- demonstrating knowledge of ways to encourage active involvement of families of English language learners in the instructional program
- applying methods of facilitating communication between the school and families of English language learners
- analyzing the potential uses of home and community resources in the ESOL program
- recognizing the appropriate use of translators, interpreters, and cultural mediators

SUBAREA IV—DEVELOPING ENGLISH LANGUAGE PROFICIENCY ACROSS THE CURRICULUM: CONSTRUCTED-RESPONSE ASSIGNMENT

The content to be addressed by the constructed-response assignment is described in Subarea II, Objectives 7–12.

HOW TO TAKE A TEST

You have studied long, hard and conscientiously.

With your official admission card in hand, and your heart pounding, you have been admitted to the examination room.

You note that there are several hundred other applicants in the examination room waiting to take the same test.

They all appear to be equally well prepared.

You know that nothing but your best effort will suffice. The "moment of truth" is at hand: you now have to demonstrate objectively, in writing, your knowledge of content and your understanding of subject matter.

You are fighting the most important battle of your life—to pass and/or score high on an examination which will determine your career and provide the economic basis for your livelihood.

What extra, special things should you know and should you do in taking the examination?

I. YOU MUST PASS AN EXAMINATION

A. WHAT EVERY CANDIDATE SHOULD KNOW
Examination applicants often ask us for help in preparing for the written test. What can I study in advance? What kinds of questions will be asked? How will the test be given? How will the papers be graded?

B. HOW ARE EXAMS DEVELOPED?
Examinations are carefully written by trained technicians who are specialists in the field known as "psychological measurement," in consultation with recognized authorities in the field of work that the test will cover. These experts recommend the subject matter areas or skills to be tested; only those knowledges or skills important to your success on the job are included. The most reliable books and source materials available are used as references. Together, the experts and technicians judge the difficulty level of the questions.
Test technicians know how to phrase questions so that the problem is clearly stated. Their ethics do not permit "trick" or "catch" questions. Questions may have been tried out on sample groups, or subjected to statistical analysis, to determine their usefulness.
Written tests are often used in combination with performance tests, ratings of training and experience, and oral interviews. All of these measures combine to form the best-known means of finding the right person for the right job.

II. HOW TO PASS THE WRITTEN TEST

A. BASIC STEPS

1) Study the announcement

How, then, can you know what subjects to study? Our best answer is: "Learn as much as possible about the class of positions for which you've applied." The exam will test the knowledge, skills and abilities needed to do the work.

Your most valuable source of information about the position you want is the official exam announcement. This announcement lists the training and experience qualifications. Check these standards and apply only if you come reasonably close to meeting them. Many jurisdictions preview the written test in the exam announcement by including a section called "Knowledge and Abilities Required," "Scope of the Examination," or some similar heading. Here you will find out specifically what fields will be tested.

2) Choose appropriate study materials

If the position for which you are applying is technical or advanced, you will read more advanced, specialized material. If you are already familiar with the basic principles of your field, elementary textbooks would waste your time. Concentrate on advanced textbooks and technical periodicals. Think through the concepts and review difficult problems in your field.

These are all general sources. You can get more ideas on your own initiative, following these leads. For example, training manuals and publications of the government agency which employs workers in your field can be useful, particularly for technical and professional positions. A letter or visit to the government department involved may result in more specific study suggestions, and certainly will provide you with a more definite idea of the exact nature of the position you are seeking.

3) Study this book!

III. KINDS OF TESTS

Tests are used for purposes other than measuring knowledge and ability to perform specified duties. For some positions, it is equally important to test ability to make adjustments to new situations or to profit from training. In others, basic mental abilities not dependent on information are essential. Questions which test these things may not appear as pertinent to the duties of the position as those which test for knowledge and information. Yet they are often highly important parts of a fair examination. For very general questions, it is almost impossible to help you direct your study efforts. What we can do is to point out some of the more common of these general abilities needed in public service positions and describe some typical questions.

1) General information

Broad, general information has been found useful for predicting job success in some kinds of work. This is tested in a variety of ways, from vocabulary lists to questions about current events. Basic background in some field of work, such as sociology or economics, may be sampled in a group of questions. Often these are principles which have become familiar to most persons through exposure rather than through formal training. It is difficult to advise you how to study for these questions; being alert to the world around you is our best suggestion.

2) Verbal ability

An example of an ability needed in many positions is verbal or language ability. Verbal ability is, in brief, the ability to use and understand words. Vocabulary and grammar tests are typical measures of this ability. Reading comprehension or paragraph interpretation questions are common in many kinds of civil service tests. You are given a paragraph of written material and asked to find its central meaning.

IV. KINDS OF QUESTIONS

1. Multiple-choice Questions

Most popular of the short-answer questions is the "multiple choice" or "best answer" question. It can be used, for example, to test for factual knowledge, ability to solve problems or judgment in meeting situations found at work.

A multiple-choice question is normally one of three types:
- It can begin with an incomplete statement followed by several possible endings. You are to find the one ending which best completes the statement, although some of the others may not be entirely wrong.
- It can also be a complete statement in the form of a question which is answered by choosing one of the statements listed.
- It can be in the form of a problem – again you select the best answer.

Here is an example of a multiple-choice question with a discussion which should give you some clues as to the method for choosing the right answer:

When an employee has a complaint about his assignment, the action which will best help him overcome his difficulty is to
- A. discuss his difficulty with his coworkers
- B. take the problem to the head of the organization
- C. take the problem to the person who gave him the assignment
- D. say nothing to anyone about his complaint

In answering this question, you should study each of the choices to find which is best. Consider choice "A" – Certainly an employee may discuss his complaint with fellow employees, but no change or improvement can result, and the complaint remains unresolved. Choice "B" is a poor choice since the head of the organization probably does not know what assignment you have been given, and taking your problem to him is known as "going over the head" of the supervisor. The supervisor, or person who made the assignment, is the person who can clarify it or correct any injustice. Choice "C" is, therefore, correct. To say nothing, as in choice "D," is unwise. Supervisors have and interest in knowing the problems employees are facing, and the employee is seeking a solution to his problem.

2. True/False

3. Matching Questions

Matching an answer from a column of choices within another column.

V. RECORDING YOUR ANSWERS

Computer terminals are used more and more today for many different kinds of exams.

For an examination with very few applicants, you may be told to record your answers in the test booklet itself. Separate answer sheets are much more common. If this separate answer sheet is to be scored by machine – and this is often the case – it is highly important that you mark your answers correctly in order to get credit.

VI. BEFORE THE TEST

YOUR PHYSICAL CONDITION IS IMPORTANT

If you are not well, you can't do your best work on tests. If you are half asleep, you can't do your best either. Here are some tips:

1) Get about the same amount of sleep you usually get. Don't stay up all night before the test, either partying or worrying—DON'T DO IT!
2) If you wear glasses, be sure to wear them when you go to take the test. This goes for hearing aids, too.
3) If you have any physical problems that may keep you from doing your best, be sure to tell the person giving the test. If you are sick or in poor health, you relay cannot do your best on any test. You can always come back and take the test some other time.

Common sense will help you find procedures to follow to get ready for an examination. Too many of us, however, overlook these sensible measures. Indeed, nervousness and fatigue have been found to be the most serious reasons why applicants fail to do their best on civil service tests. Here is a list of reminders:

- Begin your preparation early – Don't wait until the last minute to go scurrying around for books and materials or to find out what the position is all about.
- Prepare continuously – An hour a night for a week is better than an all-night cram session. This has been definitely established. What is more, a night a week for a month will return better dividends than crowding your study into a shorter period of time.
- Locate the place of the exam – You have been sent a notice telling you when and where to report for the examination. If the location is in a different town or otherwise unfamiliar to you, it would be well to inquire the best route and learn something about the building.
- Relax the night before the test – Allow your mind to rest. Do not study at all that night. Plan some mild recreation or diversion; then go to bed early and get a good night's sleep.
- Get up early enough to make a leisurely trip to the place for the test – This way unforeseen events, traffic snarls, unfamiliar buildings, etc. will not upset you.
- Dress comfortably – A written test is not a fashion show. You will be known by number and not by name, so wear something comfortable.
- Leave excess paraphernalia at home – Shopping bags and odd bundles will get in your way. You need bring only the items mentioned in the official notice you received; usually everything you need is provided. Do not bring reference books to the exam. They will only confuse those last minutes and be taken away from you when in the test room.

- Arrive somewhat ahead of time – If because of transportation schedules you must get there very early, bring a newspaper or magazine to take your mind off yourself while waiting.
- Locate the examination room – When you have found the proper room, you will be directed to the seat or part of the room where you will sit. Sometimes you are given a sheet of instructions to read while you are waiting. Do not fill out any forms until you are told to do so; just read them and be prepared.
- Relax and prepare to listen to the instructions
- If you have any physical problem that may keep you from doing your best, be sure to tell the test administrator. If you are sick or in poor health, you really cannot do your best on the exam. You can come back and take the test some other time.

VII. AT THE TEST

The day of the test is here and you have the test booklet in your hand. The temptation to get going is very strong. Caution! There is more to success than knowing the right answers. You must know how to identify your papers and understand variations in the type of short-answer question used in this particular examination. Follow these suggestions for maximum results from your efforts:

1) Cooperate with the monitor

The test administrator has a duty to create a situation in which you can be as much at ease as possible. He will give instructions, tell you when to begin, check to see that you are marking your answer sheet correctly, and so on. He is not there to guard you, although he will see that your competitors do not take unfair advantage. He wants to help you do your best.

2) Listen to all instructions

Don't jump the gun! Wait until you understand all directions. In most civil service tests you get more time than you need to answer the questions. So don't be in a hurry. Read each word of instructions until you clearly understand the meaning. Study the examples, listen to all announcements and follow directions. Ask questions if you do not understand what to do.

3) Identify your papers

Civil service exams are usually identified by number only. You will be assigned a number; you must not put your name on your test papers. Be sure to copy your number correctly. Since more than one exam may be given, copy your exact examination title.

4) Plan your time

Unless you are told that a test is a "speed" or "rate of work" test, speed itself is usually not important. Time enough to answer all the questions will be provided, but this does not mean that you have all day. An overall time limit has been set. Divide the total time (in minutes) by the number of questions to determine the approximate time you have for each question.

5) Do not linger over difficult questions

If you come across a difficult question, mark it with a paper clip (useful to have along) and come back to it when you have been through the booklet. One caution if you do this – be sure to skip a number on your answer sheet as well. Check often to be sure that you have not lost your place and that you are marking in the row numbered the same as the question you are answering.

6) Read the questions

Be sure you know what the question asks! Many capable people are unsuccessful because they failed to read the questions correctly.

7) Answer all questions

Unless you have been instructed that a penalty will be deducted for incorrect answers, it is better to guess than to omit a question.

8) Speed tests

It is often better NOT to guess on speed tests. It has been found that on timed tests people are tempted to spend the last few seconds before time is called in marking answers at random – without even reading them – in the hope of picking up a few extra points. To discourage this practice, the instructions may warn you that your score will be "corrected" for guessing. That is, a penalty will be applied. The incorrect answers will be deducted from the correct ones, or some other penalty formula will be used.

9) Review your answers

If you finish before time is called, go back to the questions you guessed or omitted to give them further thought. Review other answers if you have time.

10) Return your test materials

If you are ready to leave before others have finished or time is called, take ALL your materials to the monitor and leave quietly. Never take any test material with you. The monitor can discover whose papers are not complete, and taking a test booklet may be grounds for disqualification.

VIII. EXAMINATION TECHNIQUES

1) Read the general instructions carefully. These are usually printed on the first page of the exam booklet. As a rule, these instructions refer to the timing of the examination; the fact that you should not start work until the signal and must stop work at a signal, etc. If there are any special instructions, such as a choice of questions to be answered, make sure that you note this instruction carefully.

2) When you are ready to start work on the examination, that is as soon as the signal has been given, read the instructions to each question booklet, underline any key words or phrases, such as least, best, outline, describe and the like. In this way you will tend to answer as requested rather than discover on reviewing your paper that you listed without describing, that you selected the worst choice rather than the best choice, etc.

3) If the examination is of the objective or multiple-choice type – that is, each question will also give a series of possible answers: A, B, C or D, and you are called upon to select the best answer and write the letter next to that answer on your answer paper – it is advisable to start answering each question in turn. There may be anywhere from 50 to 100 such questions in the three or four hours allotted and you can see how much time would be taken if you read through all the questions before beginning to answer any. Furthermore, if you

come across a question or group of questions which you know would be difficult to answer, it would undoubtedly affect your handling of all the other questions.

4) If the examination is of the essay type and contains but a few questions, it is a moot point as to whether you should read all the questions before starting to answer any one. Of course, if you are given a choice – say five out of seven and the like – then it is essential to read all the questions so you can eliminate the two that are most difficult. If, however, you are asked to answer all the questions, there may be danger in trying to answer the easiest one first because you may find that you will spend too much time on it. The best technique is to answer the first question, then proceed to the second, etc.

5) Time your answers. Before the exam begins, write down the time it started, then add the time allowed for the examination and write down the time it must be completed, then divide the time available somewhat as follows:
    - If 3-1/2 hours are allowed, that would be 210 minutes. If you have 80 objective-type questions, that would be an average of 2-1/2 minutes per question. Allow yourself no more than 2 minutes per question, or a total of 160 minutes, which will permit about 50 minutes to review.
    - If for the time allotment of 210 minutes there are 7 essay questions to answer, that would average about 30 minutes a question. Give yourself only 25 minutes per question so that you have about 35 minutes to review.

6) The most important instruction is to read each question and make sure you know what is wanted. The second most important instruction is to time yourself properly so that you answer every question. The third most important instruction is to answer every question. Guess if you have to but include something for each question. Remember that you will receive no credit for a blank and will probably receive some credit if you write something in answer to an essay question. If you guess a letter – say "B" for a multiple-choice question – you may have guessed right. If you leave a blank as an answer to a multiple-choice question, the examiners may respect your feelings but it will not add a point to your score. Some exams may penalize you for wrong answers, so in such cases only, you may not want to guess unless you have some basis for your answer.

7) Suggestions
    a. Objective-type questions
        1. Examine the question booklet for proper sequence of pages and questions
        2. Read all instructions carefully
        3. Skip any question which seems too difficult; return to it after all other questions have been answered
        4. Apportion your time properly; do not spend too much time on any single question or group of questions
        5. Note and underline key words – all, most, fewest, least, best, worst, same, opposite, etc.
        6. Pay particular attention to negatives
        7. Note unusual option, e.g., unduly long, short, complex, different or similar in content to the body of the question
        8. Observe the use of "hedging" words – probably, may, most likely, etc.

9. Make sure that your answer is put next to the same number as the question
10. Do not second-guess unless you have good reason to believe the second answer is definitely more correct
11. Cross out original answer if you decide another answer is more accurate; do not erase until you are ready to hand your paper in
12. Answer all questions; guess unless instructed otherwise
13. Leave time for review

b. Essay questions
1. Read each question carefully
2. Determine exactly what is wanted. Underline key words or phrases.
3. Decide on outline or paragraph answer
4. Include many different points and elements unless asked to develop any one or two points or elements
5. Show impartiality by giving pros and cons unless directed to select one side only
6. Make and write down any assumptions you find necessary to answer the questions
7. Watch your English, grammar, punctuation and choice of words
8. Time your answers; don't crowd material

8) Answering the essay question

Most essay questions can be answered by framing the specific response around several key words or ideas. Here are a few such key words or ideas:

M's: manpower, materials, methods, money, management
P's: purpose, program, policy, plan, procedure, practice, problems, pitfalls, personnel, public relations

a. Six basic steps in handling problems:
1. Preliminary plan and background development
2. Collect information, data and facts
3. Analyze and interpret information, data and facts
4. Analyze and develop solutions as well as make recommendations
5. Prepare report and sell recommendations
6. Install recommendations and follow up effectiveness

b. Pitfalls to avoid
1. Taking things for granted – A statement of the situation does not necessarily imply that each of the elements is necessarily true; for example, a complaint may be invalid and biased so that all that can be taken for granted is that a complaint has been registered
2. Considering only one side of a situation – Wherever possible, indicate several alternatives and then point out the reasons you selected the best one
3. Failing to indicate follow up – Whenever your answer indicates action on your part, make certain that you will take proper follow-up action to see how successful your recommendations, procedures or actions turn out to be
4. Taking too long in answering any single question – Remember to time your answers properly

EXAMINATION SECTION

EXAMINATION SECTION
TEST 1

DIRECTIONS: Each question or incomplete statement is followed by several suggested answers or completions. Select the one the BEST answers the question or completes the statement. *PRINT THE LETTER OF THE CORRECT ANSWER IN THE SPACE AT THE RIGHT.*

1. Which of the following is LEAST likely to be a strategy used by a second-language learner? 1.____

    A. Overgeneralizing rules
    B. The use of simple structures before more complex ones.
    C. Disregarding present tenses in favor of the perfect
    D. Overextending the meaning of words (i.e., using *long* and *short* for *big* and *small*)

2. Typically, an activity that is believed to help establish clarity in an ESL classroom is 2.____

    A. completing the semester's 1,000-word reading quota
    B. writing a 500-word book review
    C. group editing in-class essays for sentence-boundary problems
    D. writing a free-response entry into a reading journal

3. An ESL teacher helps students generate a list of questions *(Why am I writing this? Who will read it? What is the clearest way to express my ideas?)* to guide their writing and encourage them to develop the habit of referring to the questions during the writing process. This approach is most likely to help ESL students by developing their ability to 3.____

    A. assess their writing progress over time
    B. work independently to improve their written English
    C. self-correct their mistakes in written English
    D. adjust the difficulty level of their writing in English

4. The political component inherent in reading and writing is identified by the term _____ literacy. 4.____

    A. cultural
    B. functional
    C. strategic
    D. critical

5. Recently developed "alternative assessments" used in ESL classrooms are different from traditional testing in that they 5.____

    A. use scaled measurements to assess student performance
    B. use a single index to measure a student's progress
    C. ask students to demonstrate with they know and can do
    D. are more successful when used in bilingual classrooms

6. A teacher distributes to students a picture of a bride and groom leaving a church after being married. In groups, students discuss the answer to the question, "What is happening in the picture?" The groups compare their results. Probably the most appropriate next step for the teacher is to 6.____

A. introduce new vocabulary necessary for discussing the picture, such as *wedding, bride, groom, marriage, reception,* etc.
B. distribute and have the class read a paragraph describing a traditional wedding
C. have the groups report their answers to the initial question
D. ask the groups to discuss a few more pointed questions, such as *How old are the people getting married?*

7. The aspect of second-language acquisition most commonly believed to be age-related is   7.____

    A. pronunciation
    B. syntax
    C. morphology
    D. vocabulary

8. ESL teachers who produce successful writers typically   8.____

    A. avoid overwhelming students by setting aside brief time slots for writing practice
    B. give students opportunities to "publish" their work to an audience
    C. limit the number and type of topics which can be addressed in in-class writings
    D. focus on a few important types of writing (compare/contrast; exposition, etc.)

9. Which of the following concepts is NOT a component of the Freirean/ learner-centered approach to ESL instruction?   9.____

    A. Collaboration and dialogue among equals
    B. Task-based objectives
    C. Emergent curriculum
    D. Generative words and themes

10. English syntax allows syllable-initial clusters of up to three consonants, as long as the first consonant is *s*, the second is a voiceless stop, and the third is a liquid (e.g., *street*). A speaker whose native language does not permit such initial clusters may insert a vowel that breaks up this cluster, thereby making it conform to a syllable structure acceptable in the speaker's first language. The student is transferring   10.____

    A. sense relations
    B. airstream mechanisms
    C. linguistic sign
    D. phonotactic constraints

11. Benefits associated with the content-based or "sheltered English" approach to ESL instruction include each of the following, EXCEPT that   11.____

    A. the scope of instruction is narrowly focused on specific student needs for English usage
    B. motivation for students arises naturally as students become engaged in concepts of history, science, or mathematics
    C. students are allowed to focus on content or meaning rather than on the structure of English itself
    D. new information presented in class is often a catalyst for further academic and language learning

12. The students in an ESL classroom are observed to be using inappropriate sentence intonations when participating in a transactional activity that focuses on the skill of ending a casual conversation. The teacher's next best step would be to design an activity that targets a brief _____ activity that targets this skill.

    A. imitative
    B. intensive
    C. responsive
    D. interpersonal

13. An allomorph of the negative prefix *in-* appear in each of the following words, EXCEPT

    A. impossible
    B. illegal
    C. insincere
    D. itinerant

14. An ESL instructor has students listen to a passage, and then has them individually answer a set of true/false questions based on the passage. As an evaluation of students' listening skills, this activity is

    A. sufficient, because such items force the listener to re-evaluate and prioritize information during post-processing
    B. sufficient, because it focuses the listeners' attention onto every sentence that is spoken in the passage
    C. insufficient, because it might indicate memory rather than an understanding of main idea or details
    D. insufficient, because it does not ask the students to restate anything in their own words

15. Which of the following is NOT typically a feature of two-way bilingual education programs?

    A. The language minority and language majority students are brought together in the same class.
    B. Program goals are functional bilinguals and greater intercultural understanding.
    C. The native language of students is carefully developed through appropriate language arts and academic subject material, while the second language is being taught.
    D. Most programs exit students into an all-English classroom after a maximum of two to three years in bilingual classes.

16. A high school ESL teacher observes that some of the Lao and Khmer speakers in his classes are having difficulty in certain content areas, and would benefit from support in their native languages. He convinces the board to hire part-time Lao- and Khmer-speaking tutors to work with these students. His actions in this case demonstrate a recognition that an important role for an ESL teacher is to

    A. encourage ESL students to seek assistance to meet their individual needs
    B. promote multicultural perspectives in the school community
    C. serve as an advocate for ESL learners in the community
    D. cultivate ESL learners' continuing development in their primary language

17. Typically, limited-English-proficiency (LEP) students at the secondary level tend to

   A. lack respect for authority figures
   B. avoid asking for help, even after progress reports and other warning signals
   C. be inclined to share and help other students
   D. take a teacher's directions too lightly, or laugh at inappropriate moments

18. An ESL student, faced with a particularly difficult language structure, breaks the structure down into three separate parts, practices each part individually, and then practices assembling each of the three parts into a sensible larger structure. The student is using a(n) _____ strategy for learning

   A. social
   B. metacognitive
   C. cognitive
   D. affective

19. Which of the following is an entailment of the sentence *Oswald assassinated Kennedy*?

   A. Kennedy is dead.
   B. Oswald acted alone.
   C. Oswald didn't like Kennedy.
   D. Kennedy knew Oswald.

20. A high school ESL teacher spends much of her instructional time interacting with ESL learners about historical, sociological, scientific, and mathematical topics in a variety of ways (discussion, journals, hands-on activities). This approach is based on the idea that second-language learning is promoted by

   A. immersing learners in the target language and restricting their primary language use
   B. using specific subject matter as the medium through which the target language is developed
   C. assessing learners' language needs on an ongoing basis and addressing those needs through direct instruction
   D. structuring learning experiences to minimize student errors in the target language

21. The Basic English Skills Test (BEST), a standardized proficiency examination,

   A. focuses on oral proficiency, including comprehension, vocabulary, syntax, and morphology
   B. solicits student responses to cartoon representations that are designed to stimulate the production of specific linguistic structures
   C. is a battery constructed to measure the English language communication skills of adults
   D. measures the proficiency of non-native English speakers who will use English in the work force in commerce and industry, in particular in the international trade environment

22. The most important task of a bilingual teacher is to 22.____

    A. assist students in dual language development
    B. prepare students for standardized testing
    C. emphasize English as the dominant language for students in American schools
    D. focus on assimilating students into an English-only classroom

23. In assessing whether an ESL student is appropriate for placement in a special education 23.____
    program, the first step is always to

    A. decide which assessment tools are adequately designed to measure the student's use of language
    B. identify assessment tools that can help teachers and evaluators differentiate second language acquisition problems from real disabilities
    C. determine if a learning problem is the result of an inability to perform in the English language
    D. locate the resources necessary to help the student overcome a particular learning or communication problem

24. Which of the following is a meronym of the word *leg*? 24.____

    A. Bend
    B. Foot
    C. Flight
    D. Arm

25. Aside from the need enable communication with other English-speaking people in writ- 25.____
    ing, purposes for the teaching of writing in the ESL classroom include
    I. removing the pressure and anxiety involved in face-to-face communication
    II. reinforcement of grammatical structures, idioms, and vocabu lary
    III. frequent, intimate involvement with the new language
    IV. opportunities to take risks with the language and create beyond what is taught

    A. I and III
    B. II, III and IV
    C. III only
    D. III and IV

KEY (CORRECT ANSWERS)

1. C
2. B
3. B
4. D
5. C

6. A
7. A
8. B
9. B
10. D

11. A
12. A
13. D
14. C
15. D

16. C
17. C
18. C
19. A
20. B

21. C
22. A
23. C
24. B
25. B

TEST 2

DIRECTIONS: Each question or incomplete statement is followed by several suggested answers or completions. Select the one the BEST answers the question or completes the statement. *PRINT THE LETTER OF THE CORRECT ANSWER IN THE SPACE AT THE RIGHT.*

Questions 1, 2, and 3 are based on the information and diagram below:

An art class at an elementary school contains many ESL learners, and is taught collaboratively by the art teacher and the ESL teacher. The two teachers introduce the color blue by leading a class discussion and creating on the chalkboard the visual representation shown below:

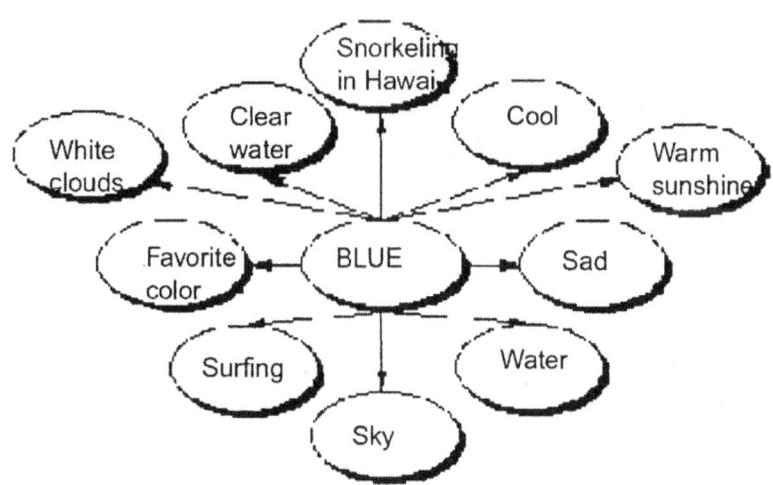

1. As an introductory activity, this strategy is beneficial to ESL learners because it   1._____

   A. allows them to develop or review key concepts or vocabulary
   B. provides them with detailed information in a concise form
   C. capitalizes on their cross-cultural perspectives
   D. promotes their confidence in producing authentic language

2. Encouraging ESL students to create their own diagrams like the one above is most likely to promote their content-area learning by demonstrating how to   2._____

   A. evaluate the reliability of information
   B. use descriptive language
   C. predict the result of a sequence of events
   D. organize and categorize information

3. A teacher could promote ESL learners' autonomy in the writing process by having them draw a similar diagram and use it to   3._____

   A. refer to the final edit of their work
   B. compare with other visual aids they've used previously
   C. generate a detailed list of topics to explore in freewriting
   D. outline their ideas before writing a first draft

4. A teacher asks his students: "What is another way to get to the freeway from here?" The cognitive process that this question is intended to stimulate is

   A. analysis
   B. synthesis
   C. knowledge
   D. application

5. Pre-writing is a strategy and activity that is typically used in ESL classrooms where the teacher takes the _____ approach to writing instruction.

   A. process
   B. free-writing
   C. communicative
   D. paragraph-pattern

6. An ESL educator studies a student's first language in order to predict and describe patterns that will cause difficulty in learning English. In this activity, the educator is employing the _____ theory of second language acquisition

   A. interlanguage analysis
   B. contrastive analysis
   C. natural language
   D. linguistic performance

7. A student writes the following: "My house has three bedrooms and a living room. A large yard is in back of the house. My mother had planted many vegetables in the yard."
   In responding to this piece of writing, the teacher should FIRST try to help this student understand the principle or technique of

   A. combining two or more related sentences into one
   B. using transitional words or phrases
   C. converting sentences into clauses
   D. placing old information before new information in a sentence

8. Which of the following paired language skill areas involve the highest degree of interdependence?

   A. Speaking and writing
   B. Reading and listening
   C. Listening and speaking
   D. Reading and speaking

9. An ESL teacher at a junior high school wants to move his students beyond conversational language, and help them develop more academic language skills. The MOST effective strategy for meeting this goal would be to encourage the students to

   A. use favorite works as models to develop their own writings in a variety of genres
   B. participate in guided readings and discussions of young adult literature
   C. identify differences in the styles of various written works
   D. evaluate information from various written sources

10. A native Arabic speaker consistently mispronounces the word *children* as *chillidren*. The speaker's error represents

    A. an incorrect peak of sonority
    B. a Creole
    C. the transfer of a phonotactic constraint
    D. a false stop

11. In a school where there are many languages and ethnic groups represented, with no clear majority within these limited-English proficiency students, the most appropriate program is probably

    A. transitional bilingual education
    B. survival ESL
    C. immersion
    D. free-standing ESL

12. Limited English proficiency (LEP) students who are mentally retarded need to have their ESL instruction sharply focused. ESL instruction for these students should emphasize

    I. social skills for community living
    II. functional skills necessary for survival
    III. generalizations form experience
    IV. memory enhancement

    A. I and II
    B. I and III
    C. II and IV
    D. I, II, III and IV

13. General objectives of a modern ESL program include the development of each of the following, EXCEPT

    A. a vocabulary for expressing oneself in different social and academic environments
    B. rule-based grammatical and syntactical construction abilities
    C. automatic control and fluency in the use of natural and accurate English language
    D. conceptual, grammatical, and syntactical forms of writing

14. In a classroom composed of a mixed-ability group of ESL learners, the MOST appropriate strategy for evaluating the progress of students at different English proficiency levels is to

    A. use multiple measures such as test scores, observations, and daily work samples
    B. assess learners only in the areas of English in which they have achieved competence
    C. select language achievement tests that have been normed on a similar student population
    D. establish a grading curve and distribute students' test results along the curve

15. Each of the following is an instructional strategy that is generally appropriate for an elementary school ESL student, EXCEPT

    A. avoiding as much as possible the use of students' native languages
    B. using authentic language at normal speed in the classroom

C. using students to teach appropriate vocabulary before using pictures or other materials
D. simplifying and adapting stories that the teacher can tell students

16. Before engaging in a grammar lesson, a group of students discuss the best way in which certain structures should be learned and practiced. The students are using a(n) strategy for learning.

    A. social
    B. affective
    C. cognitive
    D. metacognitive

17. Which of the following sentences illustrates the perfective aspect of English?

    A. He used to exercise.
    B. He quit exercising.
    C. He exercises.
    D. He began exercising today.

18. Assumptions of the whole language approach to ESL include each of the following, EXCEPT the idea that

    A. reading, writing and oral language are not considered separate components of the curriculum
    B. every day, students should read from passages that are adapted for grade-level and language appropriateness
    C. student work, especially at beginning levels, should receive much encouragement and very little correction
    D. children are expected to learn to read and write gradually and naturally, with a minimum of direct instruction

19. When communicating with parents of limited English proficient (LEP) students, it is important for the ESL teacher to understand that many immigrant families believe that the economic survival of their family depends on

    A. moving to the United States
    B. the education of their children
    C. finding a permanent position
    D. maintaining permanent resident status

20. Typically, integrated language and content-area instruction has been used by ESL educators to

    A. prepare students for requisite grade-level work
    B. develop students' academic language abilities and help them into mainstream classes
    C. prepare students for standardized testing
    D. evaluate the oral proficiency of students

21. Given what is known about the process of second-language acquisition, it is probably LEAST useful for adult ESL speakers to spend a significant amount of time attempting to

    A. control language structures
    B. perfect their pronunciation
    C. improve comprehension of speech
    D. achieve fluency

    21._____

22. The "head" of the phrase *praying quietly among themselves* is the word

    A. themselves
    B. praying
    C. among
    D. quietly

    22._____

23. In most ESL classrooms, project-based learning is based on each of the following principles, EXCEPT that it should

    A. involve students in choosing the focus of the project
    B. build on previous knowledge
    C. require students to engage in some independent work
    D. ask students to use English in familiar and comfortable contexts

    23._____

24. In terms of its place of articulation, the English [k] sound is a(n)

    A. apico-dental
    B. sublamino-prepalatal
    C. lamino-alveolar
    D. dorso-velar

    24._____

25. Principles for teaching writing in the modern ESL classroom include the idea that
    I. students should write with a specific audience in mind
    II. the teacher should serve as a coach who helps clarify thinking
    III. writing is a mechanical process that helps students to code in a new language
    IV. interaction is an integral part of the writing process

    A. I and II
    B. I, II and IV
    C. II, III and IV
    D. I, II, III and IV

    25._____

KEY (CORRECT ANSWERS)

1.	A	11.	D
2.	D	12.	D
3.	D	13.	B
4.	A	14.	A
5.	A	15.	A
6.	B	16.	D
7.	D	17.	C
8.	C	18.	B
9.	B	19.	B
10.	C	20.	B

21. B
22. B
23. D
24. D
25. B

TEST 3

DIRECTIONS: Each question or incomplete statement is followed by several suggested answers or completions. Select the one the BEST answers the question or completes the statement. *PRINT THE LETTER OF THE CORRECT ANSWER IN THE SPACE AT THE RIGHT.*

1. A successful ESL reading program will ask readers to do each of the following, EXCEPT   1.____

   A. construct purposes for reading
   B. decode each individual sentence in a passage
   C. activate relevant background or prior knowledge
   D. continually self-monitor to see if they are understanding a text

2. A teacher asks his students: "How can you use the telephone to get dinner for your family?" The cognitive process that this question is intended to stimulate is   2.____

   A. application
   B. knowledge
   C. evaluation
   D. analysis

3. The behaviorist model of learning is the source of the _____ approach to teaching ESL.   3.____

   A. Classical
   B. Direct
   C. Audiolingual
   D. Whole language

4. Limited English proficiency (LEP) students who are learning disabled often display common semantic difficulties. Which of the following is NOT one of these?   4.____

   A. Generating or recalling stories
   B. Naming verbal opposites
   C. Naming familiar objects
   D. Retrieving words from memory

5. An ESL teacher distributes to the class the following writing prompt: 5.____
   You are participating in a student exchange program with another school. Students will visit another school, and a student's home, for a period of six months. A blind student, whom you've never met or corresponded with, will be coming to your home and staying in your room. Describe the room in detail so that the student will be able to picture it, imagining that your description will be read onto an audiotape that the student can listen to.
   The theory of writing instruction being used by the teacher here is the _____ approach.

   A. audio-lingual
   B. communicative
   C. paragraph-pattern
   D. grammar-syntax organization

13

6. Most advocates of bilingual instruction suggest that linguistically and culturally diverse students should continue to speak their first language while they are learning English, primarily for the purpose of

   A. helping them to assimilate more gradually into the school system
   B. maintaining cultural ties to the families and communities
   C. better communication with language teachers
   D. encouraging bilingual development

7. In contemporary classrooms, appropriate ESL instruction
   I. integrates the skill areas of understanding, speaking, reading and writing
   II. takes the tabula rasa approach to students' prior linguistic, conceptual, and cultural experiences to build English proficiency
   III. emphasizes comprehension and morphology
   IV. provides for continued development in the functional contexts of learning and communication

   A. I only
   B. I and IV
   C. II, III and IV
   D. I, II, III and IV

8. For a beginning ESL teacher, a portfolio is MOST useful as a means of periodically evaluating

   A. the teacher's knowledge about teaching
   B. the value of a methods course
   C. how the teacher behaves in the classroom
   D. how the teacher uses his knowledge in a teaching situation

9. The following question is based on the dialogue below between two second-graders: Amy, a native English speaker, and Lan, a beginning English learner.
   1. Amy: *You want to play volleyball with us today?*
   2. Lan: (smiles and nods) *Ball yes.*
   3. Amy: (looks at Lan's paper) *What is that a picture of?*
   4. Lan: *Horse this.*
   5. Amy: *Looks like a cow.*
   6. Lan: (smiles as the bell rings) *Time for recess.*

   Lan's statements in lines 2 and 4 are not as proficient as her statement in line 6. This is most likely because in line 6, Lan is

   A. imitating speech she has already heard, rather than constructing speech herself
   B. less anxious about speaking in a context that is informal, rather than about speaking English within the classroom
   C. is more interested in the conversation, now that it has turned to a subject of her liking
   D. has taken control of the conversation, instead of responding to questions she does not fully understand

10. A learner of English, relying on experience with English morphemes, misinterprets the meaning *of discourse* as "in the wrong direction." This is an example of

   A. phonotactic constraint
   B. deceptive transparency
   C. the projection problem
   D. interlanguage

11. In an ESL classroom, the teacher is a bilingual who accepts student responses in their first languages, but responds only in English. The type of ESL program in place here is most likely

   A. immersion
   B. survival ESL
   C. transitional ESL
   D. developmental bilingual education

12. Outside of the ESL classroom, it is generally true that

   A. the listening skill is used less often than reading or writing skills
   B. most English-language experiences take place through the written media
   C. speaking is used more often than listening
   D. listening is used twice as often as speaking

13. As a general rule, a teacher in an ESL class should do no more than _____ % of the talking in the class, whether it is in English or the students' native language

   A. 10
   B. 25
   C. 50
   D. 70

14. Which of the following is a metacognitive strategy for learning?

   A. Using self-talk to persist at a difficult task
   B. The use of mnemonic devices to remember verb endings
   C. Giving oneself specific predetermined rewards for achieving certain stages of a project
   D. Self-evaluation of one's own writing performance

15. Which of the following words is a nominalization?

   A. Complement
   B. Memory
   C. Arrival
   D. Spoken

16. An ESL teacher distributes a multiple intelligences inventory among her students. The inventory is a survey with a list of many different statements, with which the students are asked to register the strength of their agreement or disagreement. On this inventory, a student who marks strong agreement with the statement "I often write notes and letters to my friends and family" is demonstrating a high likelihood of _____ intelligence.

A. verbal/linguistic
B. interpersonal
C. logical/mathematical
D. intrapersonal

17. In adult "survival" ESL programs, which of the following instructional activities would probably be LEAST appropriate?

    A. Short lesson on available community resources
    B. Practice filling out forms
    C. Pattern drills using the present perfect tense
    D. Practice speaking and reading phrases and passages with employment-related vocabulary

17.____

18. An ESL teacher engages students in a listening exercise in which they recognize questions and statements that differ only in intonation. The teacher is helping the students develop _____ skills.

    A. filtering
    B. encoding
    C. bottom-up processing
    D. top-down processing

18.____

19. The English copula is

    A. and
    B. have
    C. do
    D. be

19.____

20. A teacher wants to train students to examine the cohesive links within a piece of writing. Which of the following exercises is MOST appropriate for achieving this purpose?

    A. Distributing a cloze exercise to students, an intermediate passage of about 250 words that has every tenth word missing. Ask students to fill in the blanks with the correct words, in the correct form.
    B. Copy a good piece of writing by one student onto the board, and then have all the students copy it as a model. Later, use the same passage for practice in dictation.
    C. Have students read a passage that has all the pronouns and possessives circled. Ask the students to draw a line that connects each circled word with the word or words it refers to.
    D. Distribute a short passage and ask them, in groups, to discuss and explain why each punctuation mark is used-or give them a passage with all punctuation omitted, and have them compose a final version i

20.____

21. Which of the following standardized proficiency examinations is group-administered?

    A. Second Language Oral Test of English (SLOTE)
    B. Idea Oral Language Proficiency Test (IPT 1)
    C. Test of English Proficiency Level (TEPL)
    D. Comprehensive English Language Test (CELT)

21.____

22. To help intermediate and advanced ESL students improve reading rates and fluency, a teacher's BEST strategy would be to

    A. expand students' vocabulary by assigning challenging texts that are just slightly beyond their instructional reading levels
    B. administer timed reading tests to students each week to motivate them to read more quickly and accurately
    C. provide frequent opportunities for students to read and reread texts written at their independent reading levels
    D. encourage students to use various comprehension strategies, such as self-monitoring, predicting, and questioning

23. Which of the following is a commonly encountered drawback to the use of video as an instructional medium in the ESL classroom?

    A. There is a lack of context for learning.
    B. Added inputs-facial expressions, body language, intonation, etc. serve to overload and confuse learners.
    C. Content is inaccessible to those who have not yet learned to read or write well.
    D. Often, it's not the best means of explaining complex concepts or skills.

24. Generally, characteristics of a good language learner include
    I. strong self-discipline and reluctance to make mistakes
    II. willingness to use the language in real communication
    III. attention to forms and patterns
    IV. active approach to the learning task

    A. I and II
    B. I, II and IV
    C. II, III and IV
    D. I, II, III and IV

25. One of the most serious limitations of competency-based workplace ESL programs is that they

    A. are related to "meta-work" tasks such as interviewing and filling out forms, and do little to prepare participants for specific positions
    B. often ignore the specific language skills that are indicated by the initial needs assessment
    C. focus on isolated second-language skills and ignore participants' full social identity
    D. are inconvenient or even distasteful to workers, who are compelled to attend by their employers

KEY (CORRECT ANSWERS)

1. B
2. A
3. C
4. C
5. B

6. B
7. B
8. D
9. A
10. B

11. A
12. D
13. B
14. D
15. C

16. A
17. C
18. C
19. D
20. C

21. D
22. C
23. D
24. C
25. C

TEST 4

DIRECTIONS: Each question or incomplete statement is followed by several suggested answers or completions. Select the one the BEST answers the question or completes the statement. *PRINT THE LETTER OF THE CORRECT ANSWER IN THE SPACE AT THE RIGHT.*

1. In accordance with modern knowledge of second-language acquisition, ESL teachers should do each of the following, EXCEPT 1.____

    A. validate and integrate first-language culture and language skills
    B. provide context and action-oriented activities to clarify language meanings and functions
    C. expect and encourage errors as part of language development
    D. urge students to speak and write constructions that are just slightly beyond their comfort zone

2. All bilingual education programs recognize the need for each of the following, EXCEPT the need to teach 2.____

    A. students' primary language skills
    B. content (subject area) matter in English
    C. the history and cultural heritage of both linguistic groups
    D. English as a second language

3. An activity believed to help establish fluency in an ESL classroom is 3.____

    A. conducting e-mail correspondence with ESL students in other parts of the country
    B. discussing particular issues raised by a reading assignment
    C. small-group proofreading of in-class writing assignments
    D. reading a daily 10-page assignment

4. An advanced ESL student grows to understand the different varieties of English that are used depending on setting, relationships among people involved in communication, and the purpose of the interaction. The student has developed an understanding of the concept of 4.____

    A. register
    B. proxemics
    C. tone
    D. linguistic competence

5. Rana, a first-grade immigrant from Syria, rarely speaks at all in class, except for one-one-one conversations with a teacher. Rana has lived in the United States for six months. Her teacher has discussed this with her, but Rana's parents assured the teacher that she is also very quiet at home. The next best step for the teacher would be to 5.____

    A. engage Rana frequently in one-one-one conversations and try to persuade her that she would learn more, and have more fun, if she communicated regularly with people her own age
    B. begin to place Rana occasionally, and then regularly, in situations where she must speak in order to take part in activities she enjoys

C. continue monitoring Rana's progress, and understand that there may be cultural or personal factors influencing her rate of oral English development
D. acknowledge the parents' input, and include them in reports after beginning a referral process for special education services for Rana

6. A teacher asks her students: "How would you compare a Vietnamese city to an American city?" The cognitive process that this question is intended to stimulate is

    A. analysis
    B. application
    C. comprehension
    D. synthesis

7. Which of the following is a nasal?

    A. *V* in *very*
    B. *Ch* in *chair*
    C. *M* in *Mary*
    D. *Z* in *lazy*

8. Which of the following is a term used to denote the variations of language used by a particular student?

    A. Sociolect
    B. Patois
    C. Idiolect
    D. Creole

9. Typically, limited-English-proficiency (LEP) students at the secondary level demonstrate
    I. a discrepancy between oral and written skills
    II. a discrepancy between subject area skills in mathematics, social studies, and English language
    III. less oral participation in class
    IV. a greater dependence on teacher instructions, as opposed to one's own initiative

    A. I and II
    B. II and III
    C. II, III and IV
    D. I, II, III and IV

10. The Cognitive Academic Learning Approach (CALLA) is based on research suggesting that effective instruction for bilingual and ESL students needs to

    A. integrate language and content, and include explicit instructions
    B. look ahead toward the eventual mainstreaming of bilingual students
    C. allow students to develop basic interpersonal skills
    D. teach fundamental communication skills in a discrete sequence

11. In the ESL classroom, story mapping is typically used as each of the following, EXCEPT a

    A. summary activity
    B. model for correct English syntax and structure

C. study guide for developing routines for learner's own creative stories
D. framework for the creation of student stories

12. Whole-language educators generally believe each of the following, EXCEPT that

    A. language uses are diverse and reflect different styles and voices
    B. language is social and learned in interaction with other speakers, readers and writers
    C. spoken language is more natural than written language, and needs to be emphasized in learning
    D. if language is broken up into parts when it is taught, it is no longer language but a set of rules, patterns, and lists

13. In the word *happily*, the morpheme *ly* can be described as
    I. lexical
    II. grammatical
    III. free
    IV. bound

    A. I only
    B. II only
    C. I and III
    D. II and IV

14. Which of the following is NOT a widespread guideline for the use of pictures in an ESL classroom?

    A. Real communicative tasks can be developed by using pictures that are provided by the student themselves
    B. In order to create an audience for student writers, it's sometimes a good idea to give different pictures as prompts to different groups within a class.
    C. Pictures should often be used to generate whole-class discussions.
    D. At the beginning level, writing assignments should be limited to what students can actually see in the picture.

15. Contemporary pedagogical theory tends to support the idea that ESL learners' initial period in second language development is best spent

    A. studying simple grammatical rules
    B. studying brief English passages for discernible patterns and markers
    C. silently listening to English as it is spoke by native speakers
    D. repeating brief pattern drills aloud with the teacher

16. Which of the following features is typical of the sheltered English approach to content-area teaching?
    I. Teachers modify their language to facilitate instruction.
    II. Instruction is supported by hands-on activities.
    III. The content taught is at the same level as the content in main stream classes.
    IV. Students receive remedial instruction in content-area subjects.

A. I and II
B. I, II, and III
C. II and III
D. I, II, III and IV

17. Generally, the most important consideration in planning to assess a student's English proficiency should be whether the assessment   17.____

    A. is used for diagnosis, placement, or analysis of achievement
    B. includes measurements of discrete language skills, as well as integrated skills such as reading, writing, listening and speaking
    C. is norm-referenced or criterion-referenced
    D. uses both formal and informal instruments for measuring language skills

18. The purpose of prereading activities in an ESL classroom is to   18.____

    A. help students formulate a variety of strategies for different reading tasks
    B. extend the amount of time students spend with a text
    C. encourage students to use their background knowledge
    D. evaluate texts for implicit values and judgements

19. Which of the following English words is the best example of a polyseme?   19.____

    A. Children
    B. Second
    C. Restaurant
    D. Shot

20. The most commonly used pre-writing activity in ESL classes that use a process approach to writing instruction is   20.____

    A. freewriting
    B. small-group generation of ideas about a topic
    C. role-playing exercises
    D. individual outlining of a first draft

21. Which of the following instructional approaches is appropriate for a preschool ESL program?   21.____

    A. A classroom environment that surrounds children with printed matter-labels, charts, maps, and names
    B. Practiced dialogues between two or more students
    C. Brief, focused crayon-and-paper drills in forming letters
    D. Vocal memorization of brief phrases and sentences

22. Suprasegmentals include each of the following, EXCEPT   22.____

    A. minimal pairs
    B. rhythm
    C. adjustments
    D. intonation

23. Students in a family literacy program are asked to compare their views and cultural values with those of many Americans. Benefits associated with an activity such as this include

    I. tapping and providing a forum for discussing student knowl edge
    II. allowing students to sustain and value their own cultures
    III. providing valuable information about learners' experiences and perceptions of American culture
    IV. providing teachers with a valuable jumping-off point for contrastive analysis of English and native-language structures

    A. I only
    B. I, II and III
    C. III and IV
    D. I, II, III and IV

24. Second-language research indicates four types of relationships between oral language and reading and writing. Which of the following is NOT one of these?

    A. Discreteness of knowledge structures
    B. Dependence upon language-processing abilities
    C. Independence of different modalities
    D. Support of acquisition of literacy with speech

25. An ESL teacher is evaluating the reading performance of a student. As the student reads from a text, the teacher makes notes on his copy of the text. Printed below is a portion of the teacher's notes on the student's reading performance.

    Last night my uncle read to us from the book.
    (with markings: (C) rēd above "read to us")

    Key:
    (dog/cat) substitution
    (C) self-correction
    (and me) repetition

    The teacher's notes suggest that to confirm the pronunciation and meaning of the word *read*, the student analyzed or made use of

    A. a word root
    B. sight words
    C. word structure
    D. semantic and syntactic cues

KEY (CORRECT ANSWERS)

1.	D	11.	B
2.	B	12.	C
3.	D	13.	D
4.	A	14.	D
5.	C	15.	C
6.	D	16.	B
7.	C	17.	B
8.	C	18.	C
9.	D	19.	D
10.	A	20.	B

21. A
22. A
23. B
24. A
25. D

EXAMINATION SECTION
TEST 1

DIRECTIONS: Each question or incomplete statement is followed by several suggested answers or completions. Select the one the BEST answers the question or completes the statement. *PRINT THE LETTER OF THE CORRECT ANSWER IN THE SPACE AT THE RIGHT.*

1. An ESL teacher believes that teaching language apart from subject matter, such as history or literature, is not as effective as integrating language development and content learning. The teacher appears to subscribe, in some degree, to the _____ theory of second language acquisition.

    A. natural language
    B. discourse analysis
    C. cognitive language
    D. linguistic performance

    1._____

2. Of the following, which stage in second-language acquisition typically occurs FIRST?

    A. Using language to communicate needs or interests
    B. Building receptive vocabulary
    C. Combining semantic and syntactic formulas
    D. Speaking in short phrases

    2._____

3. A native Spanish speaker asks a classmate, in English, *Do you play any esports?* The student has committed an error of

    A. syntax   B. morphology   C. phonology   D. semantics

    3._____

4. For ESL students who are language disabled, language instruction should

    A. have both a cognitive and linguistic purpose
    B. use repetitive drilling
    C. be broken down into component parts
    D. conform to more direct, immersion models

    4._____

5. A teacher wants to give students practice in inventing and writing a narrative. Probably the best instructional aid for this task is a(n)

    A. sequenced picture set
    B. audiotape
    C. chart or graph
    D. short reading passage with large sections missing

    5._____

6. The criteria of any task within a communicative assessment would typically include performance criteria such as the
    I. speed at which a task was accomplished
    II. the number of repetitions or hesitations which interfered with communication
    III. accuracy with which the test taker incorporated formal English structures
    IV. the quality and quantity of phonological errors

    A. I and III   B. I, II and III   C. II and III   D. I, II, III and IV

    6._____

7. A high school ESL teacher makes available to students an interactive computer program called "Dear Mr. Fixit," in which students engage in a written dialogue with a computer "advice columnist." An example of a student interaction follows:

   Student: *Having a problem.*
   Mr. Fixit: *You have a problem? Tell me about your problem.*
   Student: *My Mather she is mad.*
   Mr. Fixit: *I don't understand. Do you mean mother?*
   Student: *Yes mother. My mother she is mad.*
   Mr. Fixit: *Your mother is mad. Tell me why your mother is mad.*

   The computer program is designed to help ESL students improve their social-communicative language competence by providing

   A. vocabulary for dealing with conflicts
   B. models of English sentences to use in constructing messages
   C. opportunities to engage in authentic communication in English
   D. practice in decoding idiomatic expressions

8. Teachers typically read English aloud to ESL students for each of the following reasons, EXCEPT to

   A. provide background knowledge for speaking activities
   B. stimulate the desire to read among students
   C. illustrate the use of certain syntactic structures
   D. provide a model of skillful oral reading

9. Which of the following sentences contains a verb-complement clause?

   A. I don't know whether he's coming.
   B. The idea that he is rich amazes me.
   C. I don't know what to do.
   D. The dog chased all the chickens away, and then looked to me for approval.

10. As a listening method, "bottom-up" processing begins by deriving meaning from

    A. grammatical relationships
    B. sounds
    C. words
    D. prior knowledge

11. Which of the following is an advantage associated with the language experience approach (LEA) to ESL reading instruction?

    A. teachers are able to maintain a high degree of control over classroom interactions
    B. materials match the language patterns and speaking vocabulary of the readers
    C. the focus of evaluation is almost solely on comprehension
    D. passages require sustained focus that will strengthen attending skills

12. Which of the following language behaviors is NOT typical of limited-English-proficiency (LEP) students at the secondary level?

    A. Very literal use of language
    B. Trouble retaining vocabulary or structure
    C. Command of several effective strategies for language learning
    D. Reliance on speech as the English-language medium

13. With regard to students' content-area learning, an ESL teacher's primary responsibilities include

    I. evaluating content-area courses to ensure that the curricula reflect cultural diversity
    II. helping students develop general skills and strategies that promote success in all content-area learning
    III. working closely with content-area teachers to monitor each student's academic performance
    IV. offering students support in their content-area coursework

    A. I and II
    B. I, II and III
    C. II, III and IV
    D. I, II, III and IV

14. Minimal pairs for the English phonemes /p/ and /b/ include each of the following, EXCEPT

    A. *pounce* and *bounce*
    B. *bustle* and *pustule*
    C. *brood* and *prude*
    D. *planned* and *bland*

15. An ESL classroom has many students who are literate in languages that use an Arabic or Cyrillic script. The teacher begins by giving these students exercises to develop letter recognition and sound-symbol correspondence skills. In doing this, the teacher is demonstrating an understanding that reading proficiency is related in part to

    A. the ability to use a variety of strategies for different reading tasks
    B. automatic recognition skills
    C. the ability to evaluate texts for implicit values and assumptions
    D. a clear purpose for the reading task

16. Which of the following ESL programs is MOST likely to provide instruction in all content areas in both the native language and English?

    A. Transitional bilingual education
    B. Two-way bilingual education
    C. Developmental bilingual education
    D. Immersion

17. Most educators and policy-makers in the United States believe that the first step language-minority students need to take in order to assimilate into the U.S. public school system is to

    A. stop speaking their native language
    B. enroll in special education courses
    C. improve comprehension skills in their native language
    D. learn English

18. Which of the following is NOT a benefit commonly associated with controlled writing tasks?

    A. Focused practice in getting words on paper
    B. Fewer time restrictions for teachers in designing and marking
    C. Concentration on specific, discrete problems
    D. Communication of real information among students

19. The purposes of pre-listening activities in listening instruction include
    I. providing background needed for students to understand a text
    II. activating the schemata
    III. establishing the purpose of the listening activity
    IV. focusing student's attention on what to listen for

    A. I and IV
    B. I and II
    C. II, III and IV
    D. I, II, III and IV

20. Most ESL programs emphasizing fluency require that students first have a basic knowledge of English syntax and a vocabulary of about _____ words.

    A. 300
    B. 500
    C. 1,000
    D. 2,500

21. Generally, ESL teachers have developed several effective ways of using the theory of multiple intelligences in their classrooms. Which of the following is NOT one of them?

    A. To teach to specific intelligences or correlate intelligences with specific activities
    B. To develop a better understanding of students' intelligences
    C. To help students develop an understanding and appreciation of their own strengths and weaknesses
    D. To provide a greater variety of ways for students to learn and demonstrate their learning

22. For ESL students, the most important factor in acquiring good pronunciation is usually whether

    A. practice is supervised by the teacher
    B. they can ignore the influence of their native languages
    C. speech is used as part of meaningful communication
    D. they are familiar with the words they're using

23. Research in the field of learning disabilities has shown that students may demonstrate learning disabilities in a second language when they do not in their native language. Reasons for this include the likelihood that the learning disability
    I. does not manifest itself in the native language because of specific syntactic or semantic differences between it and English
    II. may be so subtle in the first language that it is masked by compensatory strategies (vocabulary replacement, generalizing from context) that are not available in the new language
    III. has been identified by means of an instrument that is culturally biased

    A. I only
    B. I and II
    C. III only
    D. I, II and III

24. The theory of multiple intelligences is important for ESL teachers because

    A. learning a language is based on verbal/linguistic intelligence
    B. these teachers work with a diverse population of learners
    C. language instruction makes use of both verbal and visual delivery
    D. educational practices need to be designed to lead all learners to the same standardized outcomes

25. Most ESL teachers today use an eclectic approach to instruction that borrows from previous and current models. Among the principles included in these eclectic models is the idea that
    I. Subject-area content enriches and provides a cognitive base to the language classroom
    II. Students' use of translation from native language to English establishes a basis for communication
    III. language learning should be taught in both the native language and English whenever possible
    IV. listening and speaking should be taught and learned thoroughly before students undertake the reading and writing of English

    A. I only
    B. I and II
    C. II and IV
    D. I, II, III and IV

KEY (CORRECT ANSWERS)

1.	C		11.	B
2.	B		12.	D
3.	C		13.	C
4.	A		14.	B
5.	A		15.	B
6.	B		16.	C
7.	B		17.	D
8.	C		18.	D
9.	A		19.	D
10.	B		20.	C

21. A
22. C
23. B
24. B
25. B

TEST 2

DIRECTIONS: Each question or incomplete statement is followed by several suggested answers or completions. Select the one the BEST answers the question or completes the statement. *PRINT THE LETTER OF THE CORRECT ANSWER IN THE SPACE AT THE RIGHT.*

1. Limited English Proficient (LEP) students who are learning disabled often display common syntactical difficulties. Which of the following is NOT one of these?

    A. Determining if a sentence is declarative or interrogative
    B. Appropriate use of verb-tense markers
    C. Filling in deleted words in spoken paragraphs
    D. Incorrect use of quantifying information

2. Reading assessments at the intermediate level of ESL instruction would typically ask the reader to

    A. locate and state supporting facts in a passage
    B. explain the main idea of a passage
    C. demonstrate understanding of analogies
    D. make inferences based on a passage

3. The basic principle of _____ theory is the distinction between the "acquisition" of a language and the "learning" of a language.

    A. interlanguage analysis
    B. cognitive language
    C. contrastive analysis
    D. natural language

4. For a particular lesson, an ESL instructor wants to link the purpose of a piece of student writing to the forms that are needed to convey this message. Probably the most appropriate approach to use would be

    A. free-writing
    B. paragraph-pattern
    C. controlled-to-free
    D. grammar-syntax-organization

5. After conducting a unit on the past tense forms of regular verbs, a teacher begins to notice words such as "thinked" and "eated" in student writing assignments. The teacher's most appropriate response would be to

    A. circle these verbs and write a note to the student to look up and correct the conjugations
    B. cross out these verbs and write the correct forms in their place
    C. take it as a sign that students have learned what they've been taught, and make a list of these irregular verbs for a later lesson
    D. circle these verbs, redistribute the assignments to small groups, and ask them to discuss and determine what is wrong with these forms

6. Classroom environments in the natural language model of ESL instruction   6.____
   I. focus specifically on the students' language needs
   II. provide extensive error correction in both writing and speech
   III. discourage the use of the students' native language
   IV. encourage internalization of the language and meanings before structural issues are addressed

   A. I only
   B. II only
   C. I and IV
   D. III and IV

7. The most prevalent argument in favor of bilingual instruction holds that native language support is important for bilingual students mainly because it   7.____

   A. allows them to maintain communication with their family and community
   B. helps them gain a clearer understanding of content-area subjects such as math and science
   C. enhances the transition from the native language to English
   D. reinforces their cultural background

8. By the late 1990s, language and ESL instructors generally considered the Internet to be a valuable source for   8.____

   A. instructional software for both English and Spanish
   B. high-quality research
   C. early-level reading materials
   D. bilingual instruction materials

9. Which of the following is a plosive?   9.____

   A. *F* in *fish*
   B. *S* in *salmon*
   C. *W* in *wet*
   D. *Th* in *Thursday*

10. In the ESL classroom, the activity of freewriting can be used to serve the practical purposes of establishing fluency and   10.____

    A. originating themes that can act as springboards for more extensive writing
    B. giving students practice with known language forms
    C. maintaining cultural ties to students' families and communities
    D. introducing new and different language structures to the writing process

11. In taking the pragmatic approach to writing, it is important for the teacher to provide opportunities for students to see writing as a(n)   11.____

    A. skill that can be mastered through careful study of rules and guidelines
    B. social tool
    C. important means of obviating academic achievement
    D. mechanical exercise

12. A teacher wants to familiarize students with the classifications systems that exist within the English language. Which of the following exercises is probably most appropriate for achieving this purpose?

    A. Discussion
    B. Traditional grammar studies of individual sentences
    C. List-making
    D. Dictation

13. Which of the following sentences contains an ellipsis?

    A. Jerry wants me to go to the concert with him, but I can't.
    B. Who was that I saw in the library yesterday?
    C. The football game is scheduled for Saturday.
    D. Most are in favor of the ballot measure, but some are not.

14. Research suggests that when teaching multicultural literature, teachers can best ensure student learning by

    A. allowing students to choose materials themselves
    B. bringing authors in to visit the classroom
    C. allowing students to read stories in their native language
    D. providing each student with individual attention

15. Second-language research indicates that the most important factor in improving vocabulary is

    A. frequency of practice
    B. the learner's proven retrieval skills
    C. similarity of drills
    D. relevant, contextualized input

16. Typically, an ESL teacher can infer that a student is NOT reading fluently when the student is observed to

    A. read out loud to himself
    B. stop reading periodically and attempt to predict what will appear later in the text
    C. preview the headings and illustrations before reading the text
    D. vary reading speed or stop to underline or highlight certain passages

17. Research indicates that the most significant differences in the first- and second-language acquisition processes exist in the area of

    A. cognitive development
    B. interlanguage
    C. sequence of form acquisition
    D. creative or rule-based construction

18. Jorge, an ESL student, has been earning low scores on his tests in ninth-grade algebra. He tells his ESL teacher that it's hard to understand the algebra teacher, and that the textbook is confusing. His ESL teacher decides to consult with the algebra teacher. The FIRST step the ESL teacher should take in the meeting is to

A. invite the algebra teacher to observe the ESL teacher conduct a lesson, so that the algebra teacher can feel more comfortable working with Jorge
B. consult with the algebra teacher to determine which materials she uses and ask permission to observe Jorge in class
C. provide the algebra teacher with copies of articles explaining recent research on ESL learning and ESL teaching methodology
D. recommend that the algebra teacher attend a professional workshop on applying ESL strategies in content-area subjects

19. Which of the following ESL programs is perceived by most school personnel, parents and students as a remedial class for students with learning and language problems?

    A. Developmental bilingual education
    B. Pull-out ESL
    C. Immersion
    D. Intensive ESL

20. The reader's "schema" is identified as important in the _____ approach to reading.

    A. critical literacy
    B. phonics
    C. psycholinguistic
    D. symbolic

21. In terms of semantic role, the *notice* in *Yesterday Jill received an overdue notice from the library* is a(n)

    A. theme
    B. agent
    C. instrument
    D. patient

22. Which of the following is a "bottom-up" approach to reading instruction?

    A. Psycholinguistic
    B. Critical literacy
    C. Phonics
    D. Interactive

23. "Unvoiced" sounds in the English language include
    I. [s]
    II. [z]
    III. [b]
    IV. [n]

    A. I only
    B. I and II
    C. III only
    D. III and IV

24. Which of the following learning goals is most appropriate for an intermediate ESL program?

    A. Writing guided compositions
    B. Being able to discriminate and produce sounds of English and basic intonation patterns
    C. Reading short selections of prose and poetry
    D. Using reference materials

25. Effective ways of promoting ESL learners' respect for their own culture include
    I. communicating high expectations for academic performance to all students
    II. using activities that encourage students to learn about other cultures
    III. using resources from students' homes and communities in teaching academic content and skills
    IV. encouraging learners to use their home language to support their school learning

    A. I only
    B. I, II and IV
    C. III and IV
    D. I, II, III and IV

KEY (CORRECT ANSWERS)

1.	D	11.	B
2.	B	12.	C
3.	D	13.	A
4.	D	14.	A
5.	C	15.	D
6.	C	16.	A
7.	C	17.	A
8.	D	18.	B
9.	B	19.	B
10.	A	20.	C

21. A
22. C
23. A
24. C
25. C

TEST 3

DIRECTIONS: Each question or incomplete statement is followed by several suggested answers or completions. Select the one the BEST answers the question or completes the statement. *PRINT THE LETTER OF THE CORRECT ANSWER IN THE SPACE AT THE RIGHT.*

1. In classrooms where the teachers adopts the communicative approach to writing instruction, the FIRST step in any writing activity is to 1.____

    A. decide the form that the piece will take and draft a brief outline
    B. determine the audience for whom the piece is being written
    C. compare ideas with other students
    D. brainstorm a list of elements that will be included in the piece

2. A major focus in an ESL classroom is student correspondence, through conversation, letter writing, and e-mail with native speakers of English. This aspect of instruction demonstrates an adherence to the_____ theory of second-language acquisition 2.____

    A. interlanguage analysis
    B. cognitive language
    C. communicative language
    D. error analysis

3. Instructional activities that focus on pronunciation skills typically begin with 3.____

    A. listening discrimination activities
    B. description and analysis of the targeted pronunciation feature
    C. communicative practice
    D. guided practice and feedback

4. Which of the following types of bilingual instruction is normally considered to be "subtractive" in nature? 4.____

    A. Transitional
    B. One-way immersion
    C. Developmental
    D. Two-way immersion

5. *Me want cookie* is an example of 5.____

    A. telegraphic speech
    B. idiolect
    C. phontactic constraint
    D. proto-language

6. A teacher wants to give students practice in listening carefully and paying attention to inflections, as well as to the mechanics of spelling, punctuation, and capitalization. The most appropriate activity for achieving these purposes is 6.____

    A. copying written texts that are read aloud
    B. a dictation exercise
    C. composing a written response to a videotaped conversation
    D. sentence expanding and recombination

7. Which of the following learning goals is most appropriate for a beginning ESL program?

   A. Recognizing cause and effect
   B. Draw inferences and conclusions based on oral communication
   C. Perceive organization and the use of contextual clues
   D. Expanding vocabulary through the use of idiomatic expression

8. The most effective and frequently used strategy used in ESL classrooms to make new language comprehensible to students is

   A. contrastive analysis
   B. concrete referents
   C. aural-oral practice
   D. repeated repetition

9. A native Spanish speaker, in his auto shop class, asks a classmate for a pliers by saying *Please hand me the forceps.* The sentence demonstrates an error of

   A. syntax
   B. morphology
   C. phonology
   D. semantics

10. Generally, each of the following is a useful approach to using cloze activities in the ESL classroom, EXCEPT

    A. having students create their own cloze passages
    B. having students fill in deletions both orally and in writing
    C. deleting words or structures at regular intervals, such as every fifth word
    D. providing a synonym as a clue for each deleted item

11. For limited English proficient (LEP) students, the writing-as-process model involves the benefit of

    A. expanding vocabulary, by having students interact and discuss assignments in English
    B. additional practice in language semantics and structures
    C. reducing embarrassment, by keeping most mistakes out of view of most classmates
    D. reducing frustration, by making the editing for punctuation and grammar only one of many discrete steps involved in creating a text

12. To promote his ESL learners' cognitive and linguistic development, a teacher encourages their involvement in a wide variety of creative projects (book reviews for the library, published interviews with school staff and community members, etc.). By using this instructional approach, the teacher is demonstrating the cognitive and linguistic principle that

    A. in order to develop knowledge, students must first receive understandable written and oral messages
    B. intellectual development and language acquisition are mutually reinforced through reading, discussing, and problem solving

C. students acquire language and content knowledge first, and then apply them to reading and problem solving
D. students have an innate capacity to solve problems, acquire knowledge, and develop written language

13. Which of the following is a "loan word"?

    A. Stolen
    B. Military
    C. Yogurt
    D. Sun

14. Which of the following strategies is NOT recommended for helping students develop reading skills in English?

    A. Concentration on one genre at a time
    B. Continuous reinforcement of oral language development
    C. Teaching tactics for figuring out word or phrase meanings
    D. Expanding student vocabulary

15. The most frequent criticism of listening assessments typical of ESL classrooms today is that the tests

    A. reinforce a passive learning style
    B. usually ask students to perform more than one task at once
    C. measure memorization, rather than comprehension
    D. do not use the kind of language used in everyday communication

16. The most significant difference between a conversational ESL classroom and traditional second-language classrooms is that it

    A. separates language skills into discrete categories
    B. emphasizes reading and writing mastery before oral communication
    C. focuses on the skills language learners already have, rather than what they lack
    D. emphasizes mastery of oral language before the introduction of reading and writing

17. Which of the following is NOT a type of free-standing ESL program?

    A. Transitional
    B. Intensive
    C. Pull-out
    D. Holistic

18. Of the following, the most effective way for an ESL teacher to facilitate the education of an increasingly culturally diverse student body is to

    A. learn the native language(s) of their students
    B. host weekly parent-teacher conferences
    C. closely observe students' families and communities
    D. attend frequent workshops on bilingual education

19. Common purposes for a period of "delayed production" at the beginning of an ESL course include
    I. giving the teacher time to evaluate the students' targeted skills for speech production
    II. giving the students an opportunity to store information in their memories
    III. sparing students the trauma of task overload
    IV. sparing students the possibility of making embarrassing mis takes

    A. I, II and IV
    B. II only
    C. II and III
    D. I, II, III and IV

20. Which of the following sentences illustrates the inchoative aspect of English?

    A. She was dieting.
    B. She kept dieting.
    C. She dieted.
    D. She started dieting yesterday.

21. Which of the following approaches to ESL instruction is ideal for learners with well-developed speaking skills but low-level literacy skills?

    A. Natural language
    B. Two-way bilingual
    C. Total physical response (TPR)
    D. Language experience approach (LEA)

22. The extent to which ESL teachers are successful in teaching good listening and speaking skills to students is decided largely by their ability to

    A. persuade students to spend a good deal of time practicing outside the classroom
    B. introduce many guest speakers to model English conversation, prompting study of both verbal and nonverbal cues
    C. bring about the students' active participation, requiring them to choose among relevant lexical and syntactical content
    D. help students internalize formal rules of grammar and syntax

23. In terms of its place of articulation, the English [n] sound is a(n)

    A. lamino-alveolar
    B. apico-dental
    C. dorso-velar
    D. sublamino-prepalatal

24. The total physical response (TPR) approach to ESL instruction is characterized by each of the following, EXCEPT the

    A. demonstration of understanding through action
    B. development of comprehension before speech
    C. use of command-and-response
    D. development of new vocabulary through student presentation

25. Before testing and labeling an ESL student as a learning disabled, other reasons for expected lack of progress (lack of effective study habits, attendance problems, interference from the native language, etc.) should be considered. It is generally true that compared to real learning disabilities, these behaviors or problems will

    A. be likely to result in socially inappropriate behaviors in class
    B. affect all areas of learning, rather than be limited to a specific area
    C. be related to problems in the student's central nervous system
    D. create serious difficulties in acquiring and using important communication and reasoning skills

25.____

KEY (CORRECT ANSWERS)

1.	B	11.	D
2.	C	12.	B
3.	B	13.	C
4.	B	14.	A
5.	A	15.	A
6.	B	16.	C
7.	B	17.	A
8.	B	18.	C
9.	D	19.	C
10.	C	20.	D

21.	D
22.	C
23.	A
24.	D
25.	B

TEST 4

DIRECTIONS: Each question or incomplete statement is followed by several suggested answers or completions. Select the one the BEST answers the question or completes the statement. *PRINT THE LETTER OF THE CORRECT ANSWER IN THE SPACE AT THE RIGHT.*

1. Pragmatic writing in a classroom generally involves each of the following concerns, EXCEPT

    A. which of several forms a particular piece should take
    B. the type of information students need to communicate
    C. why students need to write a particular piece
    D. the most appropriate writing medium

    1.____

2. Which of the following learning goals is most appropriate for an advanced ESL program?

    A. Writing personal letters and book reports
    B. Acquiring knowledge of a new cultural environment
    C. Refining production of the sounds of English
    D. Comprehending reading passages with interpretive expression

    2.____

3. Which of the following in-class exercises would be MOST useful for the development of vocabulary?

    A. Role playing
    B. Semantic mapping
    C. Natural approach techniques
    D. Content-based language tasks

    3.____

4. Which of the following English sounds is classified as a sonorant?

    A. [f]
    B. [b]
    C. [k]
    D. [m]

    4.____

5. Copying can be a useful technique for teaching writing to ESL students when students

    A. are advanced ESL learners who need to master a particularly difficult form
    B. will need the copied text in some way to carry out a classroom activity
    C. need to practice one or two specific forms or mechanical elements
    D. will later be asked to read aloud the passage that is being copied

    5.____

6. Whole-language approaches to teaching ESL, such as "Fluency First," differ from more traditional methods in several ways. Which of the following is NOT a characteristic of these whole-language approaches?

    A. Much more extensive reading and writing requirements, even for low-proficiency students.
    B. Teachers are more active in classroom activities.
    C. Grammar is not taught separately, but within the contexts of students' own writings.
    D. Readings are authentic texts that are not adapted for ESL readers.

    6.____

7. Which of the following approaches to ESL instruction is MOST appropriate for students with academic, employment, or basic survival goals?

   A. Developmental bilingual
   B. Competency-based education
   C. Language experience approach (LEA)
   D. Natural language

8. In designing instruction for ESL students with learning disabilities, a teacher should use each of the following guidelines, EXCEPT

   A. provide constant structure and multisensory review
   B. include opportunities to employ several different learning strategies
   C. simplify language, but not content
   D. reinforce main ideas and concepts through constant and precise repetition

9. A group of ESL students is asked to read a short passage and then meet as a group to compare the author's position on a topic to their own. The teacher is working with the students to develop _____ literacy.

   A. critical
   B. discursive
   C. functional
   D. cultural

10. Which of the following standardized proficiency examinations is a criterion-referenced test designed to assess the language dominance, proficiency, and growth of students in grades K-12?

    A. Basic Inventory of Natural Language (BINL)
    B. Language Assessment Scales (LAS)
    C. Test of English Proficiency Level (TEPL)
    D. Basic English Skills Test (BEST)

11. The current thinking on the proper sequence of instruction for English reading, writing, listening and speaking skills is that

    A. the skills are so interdependent that they should be taught simultaneously, in some form, from the beginning
    B. it is usually helpful to concentrate on listening first, then to move toward speaking, reading, and finally writing
    C. the sequence should depend on whether the student is primary a visual or auditory learner
    D. in order to save students from an initial embarrassment that might discourage further learning, it's best to study a language graphically (through reading and writing) before forcing students to speak in class

12. In terms of semantic role, the word *dog* in *Fred bathed his mother's dog* is a(n)

    A. patient
    B. theme
    C. agent
    D. instrument

13. In reference to listening skills, "top-down processing" refers to a listener's deriving meaning through

    A. stress, rhythm, and intonation
    B. the speaker's body language
    C. phonemes and morphemes
    D. background knowledge and global understanding

14. Which of the following statements about holistic ESL programs is FALSE?

    A. Students receive a short and intensive English program, including instruction in academic language.
    B. Instructional designs use the curriculum content areas.
    C. Pedagogical focus is typically removed from the English language itself.
    D. They are most appropriate for schools with large populations of LEP students.

15. Students in a high school math class frequently discuss mathematical concepts in small groups, working on student-generated problems that have a variety of possible correct answers. The approach is most likely to promote learning among ESL students in the class by

    A. providing opportunities to develop and use critical thinking skills
    B. allowing carefully structured knowledge to be transferred directly from teacher to students
    C. breaking down concepts into discrete parts that are easy for learners to comprehend
    D. giving students with opportunities for individual skills practice

16. A teacher is helping students through one of their first extended writing assignments, using a process approach. In this model of instruction, it is MOST appropriate for students to focus their attention to elements such as grammar, spelling, and punctuation during the _____ phase.

    A. pre-writing
    B. drafting
    C. revising
    D. editing

17. Most research in second-language acquisition indicates that the most important individual variable in foreign language learning is

    A. cognitive style
    B. aptitude
    C. personality
    D. motivation

18. Which of the following is a term related to the physical distances maintained by speakers of different languages as they speak to each other or others?

    A. Proxemics
    B. Holophrastics
    C. Proximity norms
    D. Linguistic intervals

19. Which of the following instructional tools is MOST appropriate for helping learners to see relationships among ideas of particular topics?

    A. Role playing
    B. Cloze activity
    C. Decision tree
    D. Semantic mapping

20. In designing a family literacy project, an ESL teacher hopes to make use of the multi-directional learning inherent in the process. Which of the following activities is MOST appropriate for use in this approach?

    A. Using elders' storytelling as the basis for a lesson
    B. Comparing English language structures to their native-language counterparts
    C. Having family members respond as a group to video segments drawn from American media
    D. Family members working together to read and decode a short reading passage

21. Which of the following verbs serves as a "dummy" auxiliary in English?

    A. Be
    B. Do
    C. Can/Could
    D. Have

22. The main rationale for using project-based instruction in ESL learning is that it

    A. helps students to practice and apply academic English language in an authentic setting
    B. helps students produce richer material, because they are in collaboration with others who share their native language and culture
    C. relates the English used in class to the English used in important real-life situations
    D. turns the primary focus of instruction away from the English language itself

23. Each of the following approaches to ESL instruction is based on the cognitive model of learning, EXCEPT the_____ approach.

    A. natural language
    B. whole language
    C. communicative
    D. aural-oral

24. Which of the following is an advantage associated with the language experience approach (LEA) to ESL writing instruction?

    A. Students gain confidence as they see their own oral work used as the basis for a written lesson
    B. Students are not made to speak until it's clear that they understand important elements of English
    C. Content-area subject matter is used to provide an environment for language instruction, taking the focus off the English language itself
    D. Through role-playing and dialogues, students are made to feel freer to express emotions and experiences

25. The main advantage of using peer journals with ESL students is that they provide 25.____
    A. practice in standard writing conventions
    B. writing fluency
    C. numerous personal teacher responses to student entries
    D. a receptive and usually non-threatening audience for student writings

KEY(CORRECT ANSWERS)

1. A
2. D
3. B
4. D
5. B

6. B
7. B
8. D
9. A
10. A

11. A
12. A
13. D
14. A
15. A

16. D
17. D
18. A
19. D
20. A

21. B
22. C
23. D
24. A
25. D

EXAMINATION SECTION

TEST 1

DIRECTIONS: Each question or incomplete statement is followed by several suggested answers or completions. Select the one that BEST answers the question or completes the statement. *PRINT THE LETTER OF THE CORRECT ANSWER IN THE SPACE AT THE RIGHT.*

1. Which of the following sentences is written in the passive voice?
    A. My best friend saw the play.
    B. The play was seen by many people.
    C. I could see the play tomorrow night.
    D. Several critics have seen the play.

    1._____

2. Use the sentences below to answer the question that follows:

    Pardon me, sir, but would you
    mind opening the window?
    Open the window, will ya, buddy?
    Open the window now.
    Gee, it's hot in here.

    Together, these utterances illustrate which of the following important aspects of language use?
    A. Monitoring
    B. Dialect
    C. Morphology
    D. Register

    2._____

For questions 3 and 4, use the dialogue below between a teacher and an ESOL student to answer the two questions that follow:

Teacher: What did you do last night?
Student: I goed play bowling.
Teacher: [enthusiastically] Oh, you went bowling? [gestures rolling a ball]
Student: Yes, I goed bowling.
Teacher: Was it fun? Tell me about it!

3. The student's past tense error in this conversation is an example of which of the following natural phenomena that occurs during the early phases of both first- and second-language acquisition?
    A. Performance errors
    B. Overgeneralization
    C. Inflected forms
    D. Transformation

    3._____

4. In this interaction, the teacher is most likely trying to
   A. convey the patterns of verb conjugation in English
   B. provide correct verb forms by directly pointing out the student's mistake
   C. check the student's level of listening comprehension
   D. encourage the student to develop fluency without overt attention to form

   4._____

5. Which of the following identifies an underlying principle of the communicative approaches to the instruction of English language learners?
   A. Students develop skills in English by mastering the written grammar of the language
   B. Students should follow a step-by-step progression of English instruction from simpler to more difficult tasks
   C. Students should have repeated exposure to accurate models of oral English
   D. Students develop English language skills by negotiating meaning in interactions with other people

   5._____

6. To promote a positive learning environment in the ESOL classroom, which of the following attitudes would be best for an ESOL teacher to communicate to students?
   A. Learning a new language does not mean giving up the languages they already know
   B. Developing English language skills will be essential for success in their adult lives
   C. They must learn science and other subjects even if English is not their first language
   D. A new language can be learned very quickly if they work hard in class

   6._____

7. A new student, Hang, enters an eight-grade ESOL class. She would like to make the transition into a mainstream class, but the report from her previous school indicates that her ability to write in English is weak. Which of the following activities would best help the ESOL teacher determine if Hang's English writing skills are adequately developed for the varied demands of mainstream classes?
   A. Have Hang assemble a collection of in-class and outside-class writing samples over several days
   B. Ask Hang to write informally in a journal every day for a week about her daily life
   C. Have Hang write a comparison/contrast essay on an assigned topic in 30 minutes
   D. Give Hang a dictation of at least 200 words from a mainstream textbook

   7._____

8. In which of the following listening situations would English language learners typically have to contend with the greatest degree of *context-reduced* language?
    A. Music lesson for learning to play the clarinet
    B. Classroom lecture about the history of the Erie Canal
    C. Televised weather report from a local news program
    D. Demonstration of how to follow a recipe to bake a pie

9. An ESOL teacher plans to use miscue analysis to learn more about the reading proficiency of an English language learner. This analysis would be most helpful in providing the teacher with information about the
    A. grade level at which the student is presently reading
    B. degree of first-language interference the student is experiencing
    C. genres of literature the student prefers to read
    D. strategies the student is using to decode and comprehend a text

10. A high school ESOL teacher creates a holistic scoring system to assess sets of papers written by English language learners. Using this form of writing assessment is most appropriate when a teacher wants to evaluate the students'
    A. ability to communicate ideas through their writing
    B. progress in expanding their English language vocabulary
    C. development of personal style or voice in their writing
    D. mastery of English punctuation and mechanics

11. An ESOL teacher has students with intermediate-level English proficiency read several chapter books from a particular series. Each book features the escapades of a group of characters who are neighbors along a country road. Engaging students with this sort of children's literature will promote the students' English language proficiency primarily because it
    A. gives them a genre of fiction to read that is well within the range of their skills
    B. provides them with a clearer understanding of sequence in narrative form
    C. encourages them to feel that they are successful readers each time they finish a book
    D. helps them build context from book to book to support their reading comprehension

12. The ESOL teachers at a high school make efforts to learn about the home language and culture of the English language learners they serve. The ESOL teachers could most appropriately use the linguistic and cultural information they gather to support the students' learning in content-area classes by
    A. providing experiences that enable students to make connections and understand new concepts
    B. guiding students toward meeting the instructional and social expectations of the school
    C. showing content-area teachers why the students may be having difficulties in class
    D. developing approaches to problem solving students can apply across the curriculum

13. According to English language arts standards, students are expected to read for information and understanding. As a *first* step toward meeting this standard, it would be most appropriate for fourth- and fifth-grade English language learners to learn how to
    A. decide which information in texts is relevant and irrelevant
    B. assess the relative value of specific facts and ideas in texts
    C. ask specific questions to clarify and extend the meaning of texts
    D. know which information in a text is factual and which is an opinion

13._____

14. As an instructional format, role-playing would be most effective for English language learners who have which of the following learning styles?
    A. Visual
    B. Tactile
    C. Auditory
    D. Kinesthetic

14._____

15. Which of the following is a fundamental element of the sheltered approach to English instruction?
    A. Helping English language learners acquire academic English as they learn academic content
    B. Using home languages for content-area instruction until students can move into all English classes
    C. Teaching English language learners about English using translation and vocabulary activities
    D. Offering students instructional activities that will reinforce their communicative competence

15._____

16. The teacher of a multilingual kindergarten class is often asked by parents what they can do to help their children learn English. The teacher always replies, "Keep speaking to your children in your native language." The teacher's response is most probably based on the understanding that
    A. children of this age are likely to imitate and retain incorrect English pronunciation
    B. language learning is most effective when the language is introduced by only one person
    C. hearing English spoken by non-native speakers reinforces syntactic errors
    D. mastery of first-language skills generally promotes successful English acquisition

16._____

KEY (CORRECT ANSWERS)

1. B
2. D
3. B
4. D
5. D

6. A
7. A
8. B
9. D
10. A

11. D
12. A
13. C
14. D
15. A

16. D

EXAMINATION SECTION
TEST 1

DIRECTIONS: Each question or incomplete statement is followed by several suggested answers or completions. Select the one that BEST answers the question or completes the statement. *PRINT THE LETTER OF THE CORRECT ANSWER IN THE SPACE AT THE RIGHT.*

1. Helping students hear the difference between similar sounds is BEST accomplished through

    A. dialogues
    B. repetition
    C. minimal pairs
    D. enunciation

    1._____

2. General phonetic training equips the teacher to

    A. speak any language easily
    B. learn the ideograms of Chinese
    C. enlist acoustics to teach pronunciation
    D. compare sounds of different languages

    2._____

3. In an attempt to produce a 'th' sound as in 'thin' a Spanish speaker may produce a(n) _____ sound.

    A. 't'	B. 'z'	C. 'zh'	D. 's'

    3._____

4. Students whose native tongue is a Romance language will all *probably* have a similar problem stemming from their native language's lack of

    A. diphthongizing tendencies
    B. the consonant phoneme /h/
    C. strong articulatory movement
    D. various back vowels

    4._____

5. Lip rounding is an ESSENTIAL part of the pronounciation of the

    A. /r/	B. /i/	C. /ae/	D. /k/

    5._____

6. Pupils should be taught that, in mastering the melody of English, the FIRST stressed syllable of any breath group is _____ pitch.

    A. highest in
    B. on normal
    C. lowest in
    D. the desired

    6._____

7. The bilabial cognate sounds that are *most likely* to be confused by the bilingual Spanish-speaking student are

    A. s-z
    B. p-b
    C. th-th (voiced)
    D. w-wh

    7._____

8. In the following, the group of words containing the SAME vowel sound is

    A. heroine, cottage, butter, lasso
    B. parade, aspirin, custody, drama
    C. university, dusk, fat, filibuster
    D. warm, sofa, hymnbook, oblong

    8._____

9. The student whose native tongue is Spanish, when making a polite request, will use a 9.____

   A. falling intonation B. level intonation
   C. circumflex intonation D. rising intonation

10. In English, a question that begins with an interrogative word should be spoken with a 10.____

    A. falling inflection or down-glide
    B. rising inflection or up-glide
    C. level intonation
    D. circumflex intonation

11. The Chinese student may consistently interchange the sounds 11.____

    A. s and z B. r and s C. s and l D. l and r

12. In order to *properly* maintain intonation in a long utterance, it is BEST to 12.____

    A. repeat it rapidly
    B. break it from the end
    C. repeat it slowly
    D. break it from the beginning

13. An initial consonant cluster which will be difficult for Spanish speakers is 13.____

    A. /pr/ B. /kr/ C. /sk/ D. /pl/

14. The puff of air which accompanies some voiceless stops in English, but NOT in Italian, is known as 14.____

    A. aspiration B. vocalic off-glide
    C. occlusion D. disjuncture

15. Spanish students will have difficulty in learning correct English sentence rhythm because under the influence of their native language they will *probably* 15.____

    A. give full vowel quality to all the vowels in English
    B. give insufficient quality to the English vowels
    C. confuse vowels and consonants
    D. over-stress too many words in the sentence pattern

16. The pitch on which the different syllables in a breath group are spoken produces the 16.____

    A. crispness of articulation B. breathing process
    C. intonation pattern D. energy of tone

17. Directing the air stream to a feather or small strip of paper is a method which can be used BEST to visually teach and reinforce correct production of the sound of 17.____

    A. m B. ah C. p D. v

18. A teacher selected a few phonetic elements, planned for the development of skills in an appropriate sequence, and carefully spaced the introduction of each element in the sequence.
    The teacher is *probably* teaching 18.____

    A. morphemes B. phonics C. verbs D. phonograms

19. When we teach syntax, we are demonstrating the correct

    A. spelling of words
    B. arrangement of words
    C. sound of words
    D. parts of speech

20. A knowledge of phonemes is IMPORTANT to a teacher of English as a Second Language (ESL) because phonemes are

    A. symbols pupils must learn to master English speech
    B. distinctive units of sound which distinguish meanings
    C. the same for all languages
    D. non-distinctive sound differences

21. Auxiliaries, conjunctions, degree words, and modals are examples of

    A. function words
    B. replacers
    C. cue words
    D. segments

22. The bulk of the vocabulary of the English language consists of _____ words,

    A. function   B. action   C. substitute   D. content

23. A Frenchman who shrugs his shoulders is engaging in the kind of communication known as

    A. cybernetics
    B. microlinguistics
    C. kinesics
    D. entropy

24. A *minimally* significant grammatical unit which contributes to the grammatical and semantic meaning of a word is a

    A. phoneme
    B. diphthong
    C. morpheme
    D. suprasegmental

25. Words in which there is NO difference except for the sound that is being contrasted are called

    A. contours
    B. minimal pairs
    C. diphthongs
    D. morphemes

26. Morphology is the study of the

    A. individual units of meaning of a language
    B. sounds of a language
    C. relationship between constituents
    D. inflections of a sound system

27. The words 'rather', 'shall', 'whenever', 'some' are examples of

    A. content words
    B. adverbs
    C. function words
    D. determiners

28. References to the surface structure and deep structure of a language are MOST closely associated with the theory of

    A. semiotics
    B. programmed learning
    C. interference
    D. transformational grammar

29. A useful rule of thumb to follow if there is more than one adverb or adverbial phrase in a sentence is to follow the pattern:

   A. Manner - time - place
   B. Place - manner - time
   C. Time - frequency - place
   D. Time - place - manner

30. According to linguistics principles, the *primary* structure of the English language is the

   A. individual sound
   B. word
   C. sentence
   D. paragraph

31. The sentence, "The inductive method makes content exciting," has a sentence pattern indicated as:

   A. S-V-IO-O   B. S-LV-PA   C. S-LV-PN-PA   D. S-V-O-OC

32. Words which are spelled the same but have different meanings are called

   A. homonyms   B. homographs   C. allophones   D. graphemes

33. There are several pairs of related words which differ only in the pronunciation of the final sound. Verb forms are voiced and non-verbs are voiceless.
    The pair which does NOT fall into this category is

   A. close/close
   B. abuse/abuse
   C. loose/loose
   D. mouth/mouth

34. Of the following, the statement which does NOT apply to the term 'phoneme' is that it

   A. is a unit of pronunciation
   B. makes up all utterances in a given language
   C. may have different pronunciations under different conditions
   D. is the system of speech sounds

35. Intonation depends on each of the following EXCEPT

   A. stress   B. volume   C. pitch   D. juncture

36. All of the following apply to morphemes EXCEPT that they

   A. are a voice signal, phoneme or group of phonemes
   B. contribute to meaning
   C. recur in different contexts
   D. can be divided into smaller units which recur with the same meaning

37. The CORRECT definition for 'cluster' is that it is a

   A. group of two or more adjacent consonants
   B. group of two or more adjacent vowels
   C. consonant followed by a vowel
   D. vowel followed by a consonant

38. The pairs, TÓRMENT-TORMÉNT and PÉRVERT-PERVÉRT, are examples of

   A. medial accents
   B. minimal pairs
   C. weak accents
   D. stress pairs

39. An example of a tag question is:

    A. How about me?
    B. Is he going?
    C. He's going to work, isn't he?
    D. Why is he going?

40. The English word "assist" does NOT have the same primary meaning as the Spanish word "asistir" or the French word "assister"; thus they are *false*

    A. homonyms   B. cognates   C. allophones   D. idioms

41. An *early* step in getting native speakers of Romance languages to recognize the sound features that are distinctive in English would involve the use of

    A. recorded speeches   B. minimal pairs
    C. monostructural approaches D. peer teaching

42. Learning our alphabet is *most likely* to be a problem for beginning writers of English whose native language is

    A. Spanish   B. French   C. Russian   D. Portuguese

43. English and Spanish are *generally* dissimilar in the position of the

    A. possessive adjective
    B. negative "not" with verb forms
    C. article
    D. direct object

44. What I can think about I can learn to talk about.
    What I can talk about I can learn to write.
    What I can write I can read.
    The philosophy expressed above is that held by advocates of the

    A. Language Experience Method   B. Direct Method
    C. Silent Way   D. Translation Method

45. A language which does NOT use verb inflection to indicate tense is

    A. English   B. Chinese   C. German   D. Italian

46. Non-agreement of adjectives with nominals in either gender or number is characteristic of the _____ language(s).

    A. German   B. Romance   C. English   D. Slavic

47. Although the Mandarin dialect is the official dialect of both Nationalist and Communist China, the dialect spoken by many Chinese students in New York City schools is

    A. Hakka   B. Shanghainese
    C. Cantonese   D. Fukienese

48. Speakers of languages other than English often have difficulty learning to generate grammatically correct English questions.
The problem is *usually*

    A. the use of question marks
    B. position and use of the auxiliaries DO, DOES, DID
    C. sentence inflection
    D. agreement of subject and verb

49. Lessons prepared in terms of performance objectives should focus on

    A. teacher personality
    B. motor involvement
    C. anticipated pupil behavior
    D. oral pattern practice

50. The construction of a mural or diorama is MOST useful in the study of

    A. structure   B. speech   C. culture   D. vocabulary

KEY (CORRECT ANSWERS)

1.	C	11.	D	21.	A	31.	C	41.	B
2.	D	12.	B	22.	D	32.	B	42.	C
3.	B	13.	C	23.	C	33.	D	43.	D
4.	A	14.	A	24.	C	34.	C	44.	B
5.	D	15.	A	25.	B	35.	D	45.	A
6.	A	16.	C	26.	C	36.	D	46.	C
7.	B	17.	C	27.	C	37.	A	47.	C
8.	B	18.	B	28.	D	38.	D	48.	B
9.	A	19.	B	29.	C	39.	C	49.	D
10.	C	20.	B	30.	A	40.	B	50.	C

TEST 2

DIRECTIONS: Each question or incomplete statement is followed by several suggested answers or completions. Select the one that BEST answers the question or completes the statement. *PRINT THE LETTER OF THE CORRECT ANSWER IN THE SPACE AT THE RIGHT.*

1. The IDEAL end result of a lesson or unit is

    A. translation
    B. reference to grammatical rules
    C. memorization
    D. free communication

2. Listening is a function that is BEST described as a(n)

    A. passive reception of a message
    B. active process of constructing a message
    C. perception based on externalized knowledge
    D. reading of cultural context cues

3. Sentence-reading practice aims to develop the learner's

    A. structural knowledge of a comparative nature
    B. eye-sweep and association of visual with sound meaning
    C. ability to read arbitrary statements independently
    D. capacity to assimilate culture and civilization

4. In order to hold the interest of most students, the teacher must plan to

    A. vary clothing and accessories
    B. prepare performance objectives
    C. vary activities, materials and equipment
    D. prepare many repetition drills

5. A test with scores which do NOT fluctuate very much each time it is given is said to be

    A. reliable   B. objective   C. valid   D. empirical

6. MOST pattern drills consist of a model, a cue, and a

    A. chain   B. stimulus   C. signal   D. response

7. When teaching tag questions, one must be sure that pupils change negative verb form to affirmative and place a _____ the verb form.

    A. noun after   B. pronoun after
    C. noun before   D. pronoun before

8. Substitution drills and slot drills should be used in the English as a Second Language (ESL) classroom to

    A. teach pronunciation   B. develop aural abilities
    C. teach syntax and vocabulary   D. replace dictation exercises

9. The backward buildup drill in the ESL class can be used as an IMPORTANT tool for each of the following EXCEPT

   A. preserving intonation
   B. teaching grammatical structure
   C. teaching sentence stress
   D. maintaining rhythm

10. The curriculum for an ESL classroom should stress basic skills in the following order:

    A. Understanding, writing, speaking, reading
    B. Writing, reading, speaking, understanding
    C. Speaking, reading, understanding, writing
    D. Understanding, speaking, reading, writing

11. When the teacher gives a minimal pair drill she should FIRST

    A. play a record
    B. go from a known sound to a new one
    C. present several sounds at a time
    D. use new words wherever possible

12. An ESL teacher who wished to emphasize the correct intonation pattern associated with a new structure would be *most likely* to use, as a teaching device,

    A. choral repetition
    B. backward buildup
    C. conversion drill
    D. chain drill

13. The affective goals of language instruction refer to

    A. listening and speaking objectives
    B. understanding speech at normal speed
    C. the students' attitudes and feelings
    D. the recognition of verb tenses

14. The ESL teacher who is aware of the contrastive differences between his students' languages and English will be able to better plan for his class.
    For example, he will know that for an Oriental child, he will have to emphasize

    A. time adverbials
    B. punctuation
    C. writing
    D. function words

15. Of the following, the PRIMARY aim of a pronunciation lesson is to develop in the pupils the ability to

    A. hear sounds accurately
    B. write sentences accurately
    C. read with comprehension
    D. give speeches

16. A language test which asks students to supply a missing word in a paragraph where the missing word occurs at predetermined regular intervals is called a _____ test.

    A. multiple choice
    B. fill-in-the-blank
    C. cloze
    D. CREST

17. *Before* teaching the present progressive (continuous) tense it is necessary to teach the

    A. past participle of verbs
    B. present tense of the verb "to be"
    C. present tense of the verb "to have'
    D. third person singular inflection "-s"

18. The classroom test BEST fulfills its function as part of the learning process if

    A. correct performance is immediately confirmed and errors are pointed out
    B. the student is challenged by contrived sentences which present difficulties
    C. the test is given without prior announcement
    D. the student's native language is used liberally

19. Developing in non-native speakers of English the ability to respond automatically in English is the ULTIMATE goal of

    A. pattern practice and drill
    B. psycholinguistics
    C. transformational grammar
    D. generative grammar

20. For ESL students the correction of specific difficulties in producing certain phonemes of the English language follows basic speech production principles.
    In order to produce an *unfamiliar* phoneme, the phoneme must FIRST be

    A. heard   B. seen   C. understood   D. identified

21. ESL teachers use group singing as an effective reinforcement and learning activity. The procedure for teaching a song is to have students

    A. repeat, listen, repeat, sing
    B. listen, repeat, read, sing
    C. read, hum, sing
    D. read, repeat, sing

22. A drill which the sentences 'I know the man' and 'He owns a garage' are combined into one sentence is called a(n)

    A. transposition drill   B. inclusion drill
    C. integration drill   D. replacement drill

23. A replacement drill focuses on substituting a(n)

    A. pronoun for a noun
    B. noun for a noun
    C. adjective for an adjective
    D. verb for an infinitive

24. A student who can speak English well enough for most situations met by typical native speakers of the same age group, but who still makes a conscious effort to avoid translating expressions and who speaks hesitantly at times, would receive an oral language ability scale rating of

    A. B   B. C   C. D   D. E

25. A beginning level class, rated e/f on the language ability scale, would be expected to learn, during the course of a semester, all of the following syntax EXCEPT

   A. articles, definite and indefinite
   B. singular and plural of nouns
   C. present perfect tense
   D. affirmative and negative statements with "to be"

26. Of the four language skills, the one which should receive LEAST attention during class time is

   A. listening   B. speaking   C. reading   D. writing

27. A test which measures the mastery of specific learning objectives is known as a _____ test.

   A. criterion-referenced   B. placement
   C. diagnostic/prescriptive   D. norm-referenced

28. A drill which offers students practice in substituting a predicate adjective for a predicate adjective is known as a(n) _____ drill,

   A. substitution   B. expansion
   C. cued-answer   D. replacement

29. Another name for the Gattegno method is the

   A. Silent Way   B. Curran Method
   C. Cuisenaire System   D. Direct Method

30. The process of changing a present tense declarative sentence to a future tense declarative sentence is known as

   A. replacement   B. expansion
   C. transformation   D. generation

31. Language dominance refers to an individual's

   A. control of the use of grammatical rules
   B. ability to speak a second language
   C. degree of bilingualism
   D. native language

32. Through the language experience approach, ESL students are taught the relationship between spoken words and the letters which represent them by FIRST learning

   A. writing skills   B. reading skills
   C. manual dexterity   D. listening and speaking skills

33. When teaching or testing lexical items it is BEST to

   A. place lexical items in a contextual environment
   B. translate the lexical items into the student's native language
   C. provide detailed dictionary definitions
   D. consult a spoken-word count for frequency of usage

34. To test the listening, speaking, and reading skills of students, teachers will evaluate ALL of the following student knowledges EXCEPT

   A. phonology   B. syntax   C. semantics   D. orthography

35. A six-year-old native speaker of English learning to read for the first time must acquire all of the following skills EXCEPT

   A. visual discrimination
   B. association of visual symbol with sound and meaning
   C. eye movement
   D. sentence sound and meaning

36. Of the following the LEAST effective way to motivate English language learning and to convey to students the meaning of a new dialogue is by

   A. using gestures   B. using visual aids
   C. dramatizing action   D. translating

37. The language-teaching methodology which views language as a system to be established as a set of habits through constant repetition of patterns and drills is the

   A. Gattegno method   B. aural/oral approach
   C. Curran method   D. direct method

38. Minimal pair drills are an *effective* way to teach

   A. inflection   B. vocabulary
   C. pronunciation   D. grammar

39. Beginning-level students who are native speakers of Chinese or Hebrew will need special practice and exercise in the reading skill of

   A. leafing   B. eye movement
   C. association   D. interpretation

40. The primary language component which must be given precedence in teaching is related to the

   A. suprasegmental phoneme   B. lexicon
   C. structure system   D. culture

41. A recommended principle of classroom discipline is that

   A. the teacher should always insist upon complete quiet
   B. teacher activity and pupil passivity are generally preferable
   C. external authority as a stimulator of controlled behavior should become progressively less needed
   D. the individual interests of the pupils should receive no consideration in the teacher's lesson planning

42. New vocabulary should always be taught in normal utterances and

   A. at the end of a lesson
   B. with known structures
   C. at the start of the period
   D. through replacement drills

43. Having native Spanish-speaking pupils hiss an initial /s/ and then leading them into the work being practiced may reduce their tendency to

    A. introduce an /e/ before the /s/
    B. aspirate the /s/
    C. glide
    D. diphthongize

44. The ESL teacher should implicitly convey the idea that

    A. English is the best language to speak
    B. the dialects that students speak are wrong
    C. there are economic and social advantages to speaking two languages or dialects
    D. the students should try to teach English to their parents

45. A progressively difficult sequence of oral pattern practice drills is

    A. repetition, reduction, progressive replacement
    B. substitution, repetition, progressive replacement
    C. replacement, repetition, integration
    D. integration, substitution, repetition

46. ACTFL, TESOL, NCTE and ESOL-BEA are examples of

    A. professional organizations
    B. standardized tests
    C. federal legislation to aid the study of language
    D. cognitive models for second language learning

47. New grammar topics should be presented

    A. at the beginning of a period
    B. with familiar vocabulary
    C. with new vocabulary
    D. through an integration drill

48. To a linguist, a GRAPHEME is simply a

    A. sound   B. letter
    C. grammatical pattern   D. unit of meaning

49. After each teacher-made test is administered, the teacher should determine which, if any, topics need to be re-taught by constructing a(n)

    A. scattergram   B. item analysis
    C. correlation test   D. T-score scale

50. The expressions "laughing up their sleeve" and "laughing in his beard" are examples of

    A. false cognates   B. idioms
    C. antonyms   D. collocations

KEY (CORRECT ANSWERS)

1. D	11. B	21. B	31. C	41. C
2. C	12. B	22. C	32. B	42. B
3. B	13. C	23. B	33. A	43. A
4. C	14. C	24. A	34. D	44. C
5. A	15. A	25. C	35. C	45. A
6. D	16. C	26. C	36. D	46. A
7. B	17. B	27. A	37. B	47. B
8. C	18. A	28. D	38. C	48. B
9. B	19. A	29. A	39. B	49. B
10. D	20. A	30. C	40. C	50. B

EXAMINATION SECTION
TEST 1

DIRECTIONS: Each question or incomplete statement is followed *by* several suggested answers or completions. Select the one that BEST answers the question or completes the statement. *PRINT THE LETTER OF THE CORRECT ANSWER IN THE SPACE AT THE RIGHT.*

1. New language learners should begin English as a second language learnings with a pattern where structure and word order resemble the native language in order to

    A. stimulate vocabulary growth in English
    B. acquire intonation patterns in English
    C. facilitate pattern practice drills in English
    D. analyze similarities and differences in the two languages

    1.____

2. The language-experience approach for the bilingual child places emphasis on

    A. the use of whatever oral language the child possesses
    B. getting word meaning
    C. the structural analysis of words
    D. accuracy in spelling

    2.____

3. When a language pattern in English permits a choice in word order, the preferred teaching methodology in working with beginning English as a second language learners would be to teach

    A. all the alternate forms
    B. only the form that resembles the structure in the native language
    C. only the form that differs structurally from the native language
    D. only the form in more common usage

    3.____

4. To give an English as a second language group needed pattern practice in changing statements to questions, the teacher would MOST likely use a _____ drill.

    A. reduction   B. substitution   C. replacement   D. conversion

    4.____

5. Of the following phrases regarding the rate at which children are taught vocabulary in a second language, the MOST valid phrase is that it

    A. should be limited to five words a day
    B. is related to cultural background
    C. depends on various factors including age, aptitude and motivation
    D. decreases as the child gets older

    5.____

6. During the course of an English as a second language lesson, if a child makes several errors in an oral response situation, the teacher should preferably

    A. ignore the errors in order to avoid inhibiting the child's responses
    B. correct each error as it occurs so that the correct form is learned immediately by the child
    C. wait until the response is completed, then point out each error so the correct form is learned by the group
    D. correct only the type of error which the lesson is intended to eliminate and ignore the others at this time

    6.____

7. The pupil of limited English proficiency learns new English vocabulary BEST when

   A. certain abstract words are taught in isolation
   B. words are taught in the context of meaningful experiences
   C. pupils are required to answer always in a complete sentence
   D. there is much repetition of words regardless of experiential meaning

8. Vocabulary development in initial English as a second language learning should concentrate primarily on the acquisition of _____ words.

   A. function   B. cognate   C. content   D. sensory

9. The pupil of limited English proficiency is BEST helped learn to speak English when

   A. he is discouraged from using his native language
   B. he has a teacher who has a knowledge of his native language
   C. he is motivated to use English within the range of his capability
   D. he is surrounded by all English speaking pupils

10. A bilingual teacher might use the technique of the backward build-up in teaching a dialogue to emphasize primarily

    A. grammatical structures
    B. intonation patterns
    C. receptive vocabulary retention
    D. phonetic analysis

11. All of the following are correct sequences of instruction regarding grammatical structures in English as a second language EXCEPT

    A. the verb base is taught before the auxiliary verb
    B. interrogatives by inversions are taught before interroga- tives by auxiliaries
    C. interrogation is taught before nagation
    D. personal pronoun subjects are taught before noun subjects

12. When a bilingual teacher conducts a language practice session, which sequence is usually advisable to follow?

    A. individual pupil; whole group; small group
    B. small group; whole group; individual pupil
    C. individual pupil; small group; whole group
    D. whole group; small group; individual pupil

13. There appear to be extensive differences between the language learning faculties of children and adults which suggest that different methods and materials are appropriate for each age group.
    With this precept in mind, which of the following is MOST valid?

    A. Children as well as adults relate speech to thoughts not immediately relevant
    B. Adults enjoy rote memorization
    C. Children are less subject to interference from their native language systems than are adults
    D. Children usually learn new words in a purely verbal context

14. Of the following, the BEST way to insure comprehension of social studies subject matter in a bilingual classroon is to

    A. provide contextual clues for word meaning
    B. give literal translations of all new vocabulary items
    C. stress colloquial language
    D. rely on work in class and avoid homework

15. In establishing rapport with students in a bilingual class, the teacher should

    A. ignore incipient behavior problems to avoid aggravating them
    B. allow pupils freedom to move around to prevent restlessness
    C. be ready to admit an error or lack of knowledge
    D. avoid setting routines and rules since they make students resentful

16. The bicultural aspect of a bicultural/bilingual program is *primarily* designed to

    A. promote understanding of American culture
    B. develop understanding of American values and to retain the homeland's traditions for familial and cultural purposes
    C. strengthen school integration
    D. fortify the study and appreciation of the English language

17. An eighth grade class is studying the various minority groups in the metropolitan area. In keeping with currently accepted thinking, the teacher's goals should be to develop attitudes and insights favoring a philosophy of

    A. the melting pot   B. separatism
    C. assimilation   D. cultural pluralism

18. When speaking English in a bilingual class, the teacher should use a consistent pattern of tempo, intonation and stress that is

    A. natural and unexaggerated
    B. similar to the students' native language
    C. deliberate and attracts attention
    D. slow and exaggerated for clarity

19. In the teaching of English language patterns to a pupil of limited English proficiency, the teacher should

    A. begin with English language patterns that are different in structure from the child's native language
    B. teach language patterns and grammatical structures in a strictly prescribed order
    C. begin with English language patterns that are similar in structure to those of the pupil's native language
    D. correct all errors the child may make in any given response

20. The teacher should help children learn standard English usage if they habitually use all of the following speech patterns EXCEPT:

    A. Failure to add "s" to present tense verbs with third person singular subjects
    B. Incorrect agreement of subject and predicate
    C. Adding "s" to form plurals of irregular nouns which do not use this plural ending
    D. Using active verbs in place of passive verbs

21. Of the following statements, the one which is correct in regard to the teaching of English to Puerto Rican pupils is that

    A. emphasis should be placed upon creating an English-speaking atmosphere, with pupils being forbidden to speak Spanish in the classroom
    B. the teacher should be fluent in Spanish
    C. Spanish may occasionally be employed to check pupil comprehension of English
    D. new words should be taught through pictures first, then through objects

22. A newly arrived Puerto Rican child who speaks English haltingly enters a teacher's class. Of the following, the procedure which is LAST in order of priority is

    A. to increase the child's English vocabulary so that he may function better
    B. to provide useful experiences which will help the child to adjust more readily to mainland life
    C. to determine the health and nutritional needs of the child
    D. to eliminate the foreign accent from the child's speech so that he will bear no stigma in his relations with his peers

23. Jose, a bilingual child from Puerto Rico, has just entered a class composed exclusively of mainland children. Of the following procedures calculated to create acceptance of Jose by his peers, the MOST effective one is for the teacher to

    A. make Jose's "expert" knowledge available to a committee working on "Daily Life in Latin America"
    B. learn some Spanish phrases and teach them to the class to make Jose feel at home
    C. place books on Puerto Rico in the class library so that other pupils can learn to understand Jose better
    D. create desirable attitudes toward Jose by having the class discuss the need for tolerance

24. All of the following are basic to the teaching of English as a second language EXCEPT:

    A. Instruction should be systematic
    B. Where possible, instruction should be based on direct experience
    C. The teacher must be aware of pupil needs
    D. Instruction need not differentiate between English and other language patterns

25. To ascertain information about a child's social relationships a teacher should administer 25.____

    A. a personality test
    B. a temperament schedule
    C. a sociometric test
    D. an S.R.A. youth inventory test

KEY (CORRECT ANSWERS)

1. C
2. A
3. B
4. D
5. B

6. D
7. D
8. D
9. B
10. B

11. D
12. D
13. C
14. A
15. C

16. B
17. D
18. D
19. C
20. A

21. C
22. D
23. A
24. D
25. C

TEST 2

DIRECTIONS: Each question or incomplete statement is followed by several suggested answers or ocmpletions. Select the one that BEST answers the question or completes the statement. *PRINT THE LETTER OF THE CORRECT ANSWER IN THE SPACE AT THE RIGHT.*

1. When teaching the sound production of the past tense of regular verbs, the verbs should be presented in _____ groups. 1.____

    A. two B. three C. four D. five

2. When the ESL teacher models the lines of an introductory dialogue for repetition, students should 2.____

    A. read the lines with the teacher from their open books
    B. repeat the lines after the teacher from their open books
    C. listen to the model with their books closed
    D. follow the lines silently in their open books

3. The linguistic approach in teaching reading emphasizes 3.____

    A. materials which have been previously presented
    B. oral language which the pupil already possesses
    C. sound-symbol correspondences in organized structures
    D. phonetic sounds of letters of the alphabet

4. The MOST effective order in which to teach oral repetition is 4.____

    A. class, groups, individuals B. groups, class, individuals
    C. individuals, groups, class D. class, individuals, groups

5. The words 'circulation,' 'digestion,' 'mineral' and 'volcanic' 5.____

    A. are difficult for ESL students to read
    B. should not be introduced in the ESL classes
    C. are scientific terms which require mastery of the English language to be understood
    D. are easy words for Spanish students to read and understand, as they know their cognates in Spanish

6. Sociolinguistic comparisons and teaching materials should include 6.____

    A. an abundance of writing materials
    B. a great deal of reading
    C. only listening and speaking experiences
    D. references to the students' background

7. When starting a beginners' class in ESL, the teacher should use 7.____

    A. a few structure patterns including many action words
    B. many structure patterns including many content words
    C. few structure patterns, many content words and many function words
    D. many structure patterns and many function words

8. The teaching of ESL to young beginners should emphasize all of the following techniques EXCEPT

    A. relying heavily on body language
    B. implementing the lesson with visual reinforcement
    C. using role playing whenever possible
    D. expecting written daily logs from each child

9. Of the following structures the one that should be taught FIRST is the

    A. exclamation   B. statement   C. command   D. question

10. The gerund found in English in such sentences as "I am ready for reading" is a DIFFICULT construction for native speakers of Romance languages because of their tendency to substitute for it the

    A. infinitive   B. prepositional phrase
    C. noun clause   D. adverbial clause

11. Of the following, the language which is comparatively UNINFLECTED is

    A. Spanish   B. German   C. Polish   D. English

12. ESL specialists have recommended that the chain drill be conducted largely

    A. at random
    B. in row-by-row fashion
    C. with students standing up in front of the room
    D. by progression from student to student around the room

13. Structural meanings in English are MOST often signaled by _____ words.

    A. equivalency   B. content
    C. the order of   D. the meaning of

14. Among the following, the BEST example of progressive development in teacher questioning is

    A. questions with OR; questions with WHAT; YES/NO questions
    B. questions with OR; YES/NO questions; questions with WHO
    C. YES/NO questions; questions with OR; questions with WHY
    D. YES/NO questions; questions with WHEN; questions with OR

15. The sequence of tenses in English *generally* requires that a verb in a subordinate clause be in

    A. present time if the main verb is WISH in the past time
    B. past time if the main verb is in present time and expresses a universal truth
    C. past time if the main verb is in present time
    D. past time if the main verb is in past time

16. A helpful way of getting students to make the distinction in the production of the vowel sounds in SHEEP and SHIP is the suggestion that they

A. read lists of minimal pairs
B. listen to lists of minimal pairs
C. keep the jaw nearly closed when saying SHIP
D. smile broadly when saying SHEEP

17. A knowledge of interlingual contrasts will alert the ESL teacher to the fact that French-speaking students need special help with

    A. abverbs of manner
    B. adverbs of time
    C. Do/Does as auxiliaries
    D. Will/ Would as auxiliaries

18. The rhythm of spoken English DIFFERS from that of many other languages because speakers of English

    A. assign about the same amount of time to every syllable
    B. assign about the same amount of time to every phrase
    C. lengthen accented syllables and make unstressed syllables comparatively short
    D. lower the pitch for most syllables

19. Italian-speaking students learning ESL may be expected to have pronunciation difficulty with the discriminating use of

    A. v and w   B. the final s   C. y and j   D. h

20. Of the following, the LEAST likely to cause difficulty to second-language learners is

    A. Today is Monday
    B. I am thirsty
    C. I have been in New York for a year
    D. It is Wednesday

21. The part of a language that is the LEAST difficult to teach: is

    A. sound   B. vocabulary   C. structure   D. syntax

22. To illustrate the use of SOME with mass nouns, the ESL teacher will NOT use a sentence such as:

    A. I wish I had some money
    B. I wish I had some news
    C. I wish I had some tokens
    D. I wish I had some time

23. As soon as two lines of dialogue have been learned in an ESL class, the teacher should

    A. have the students copy the two lines into their notebooks
    B. allow the students to play-act the lines
    C. proceed to change positive statements to negatives
    D. proceed to teach the third line singly

24. Phoneticians have discovered that the ear has to be trained: to hear new sounds accurately.
    On the basis of this assumption, the ESl teacher will *most usually* start his pronunciation lesson with

A. having the student listen for the difference in a scrambled list of words that contain two contrasting sounds
B. the practice of minimal pairs which contain two contrasting sounds
C. an explanation of how two contrasting sounds differ in the way we hear them
D. a demonstration of the production of two contrasting sounds

25. The educational concept of proceeding from the known to the unknown in an ESL class is BEST exemplified by the teaching of:

    A. ISN'T after IS in a context of interesting places to visit in the community
    B. DOESN'T after ISN'T in a context of interesting places to visit in the community
    C. DOESN'T after ISN'T in a context of job opportunities for doctors in England
    D. AREN'T after DOESN'T in a context of job opportunities for doctors in the community

---

KEY (CORRECT ANSWERS)

1.	B	11.	B
2.	C	12.	D
3.	C	13.	C
4.	A	14.	A
5.	D	15.	D
6.	D	16.	C
7.	C	17.	C
8.	D	18.	C
9.	B	19.	C
10.	A	20.	A

21.	B
22.	C
23.	B
24.	B
25.	A

TEST 3

DIRECTIONS: Each question or incomplete statement is followed by several suggested answers or completions. Select the one that BEST answers the question or completes the statement. *PRINT THE LETTER OF THE CORRECT ANSWER IN THE SPACE AT THE RIGHT.*

1. In a maintenance approach to bilingual education, the teacher must teach all of the following subject areas in the dominant language EXCEPT

    A. music and art
    B. science and social studies
    C. mathematics
    D. reading and language arts

    1._____

2. In providing English as a Second Language instruction, the teacher

    A. is aware that children usually understand the new language before they are able to and willing to express themselves in that language
    B. tries to introduce reading and writing skills concurrently with listening and speaking
    C. gives priority to teaching study skills
    D. emphasizes free reading and writing assignments over controlled language structures

    2._____

3. Once the child has learned to read in the native language, learning to read a second language should present no problem because

    A. basic reading skills are transferable
    B. the second language is easier than the first language
    C. the phonetic systems are the same
    D. the alphabet is the same

    3._____

4. A basic tenet of second language acquisition states that:

    A. The child's later control and conception of the two languages as separate systems representing distinct cultures depends upon keeping the two languages separate in teaching
    B. A second language can best be learned by a study of cognates and parallel structures
    C. The dual language approach insures the optimum learning of a language
    D. Learning a new language is essentially and principally vocabulary acquisition

    4._____

5. English language instruction in bilingual bicultural programs follows accepted teaching methodology by developing in sequence the four language skills of

    A. speaking, listening comprehension, reading and writing
    B. reading, writing, listening comprehension and speaking
    C. listening comprehension, reading, speaking and writing
    D. listening comprehension, speaking, reading and writing

    5._____

6. All of the following statements in connection with the teaching of reading to bilingual children are valid EXCEPT:

    A. Standardized bilingual tests are a true indication of the child's potential and ability
    B. Reading ability is negatively affected by meager backgrounds of experience, concept and general information
    C. Children must be familiar with speech sounds before they can master the symbols used to represent them on the printed page
    D. The syntactical structure with which the bilingual child is familiar is frequently at variance with that which he tries to read at school

7. In planning a directed reading lesson, the teacher of a bilingual class may use all of the following procedures EXCEPT:

    A. Motivate the class and awaken a desire to find out what the material says
    B. Plan a variety of objective exercises to test comprehension
    C. Pose factual questions to the class, the answers to which may be found in the text
    D. Read the material aloud to the class slowly so that all will be able to follow

8. In examining a number of readers based on the linguistic approach, the teacher of bilingual children notes that stress is placed on

    A. correct response of the pupil to each step of what is to be learned
    B. recognition of reading as a symbol-sound correspondence
    C. elimination of differences between upper and lower case letters
    D. content geared to the experiences of urban children

9. When a bilingual child uses context clues to unlock the meaning of a new word, he recognizes the word

    A. through association of its sounds with their letter symbols
    B. from its root parts
    C. from its setting in a sentence or paragraph
    D. from its configuration

10. Of the following reasons, the one which is NOT applicable to the use of the language experience approach in meeting the individual needs of bilingual children is that this method

    A. limits the word recognition skills that are used
    B. uses the existing oral language background of the child
    C. stresses the interrelationship of listening, speaking, reading and writing in the language arts
    D. strengthens the relationship between the oral and printed word

11. Of the following factors, the one which is NOT a basis for grouping bilingual children for reading instruction in a basal reader is

    A. flexibility of groups
    B. readiness and maturity
    C. language ability
    D. instructional reading level

12. A guided reading lesson in the dominant language should include all of the following elements EXCEPT

    A. reading the entire story orally to evaluate reading progress
    B. establishing background by stimulating pupils to think along the lines of the story
    C. presenting new words in meaningful context
    D. having children read silently to find answers to key questions

13. All of the following activities will help the bilingual child to achieve the goal developing work recognition skills EXCEPT

    A. developing interest in words through the picture dictionary
    B. selecting a title which best expresses the main idea
    C. developing the meaning of words in a familiar context
    D. identifying the two separate words in a compound word

14. Of the following statement regarding a child's readiness for systematic instruction in reading, the LEAST valid statement is the child

    A. speaks spontaneously and clearly
    B. is interested in the books the teacher is reading to the class
    C. has adequate vision, hearing and motor coordination
    D. shows ability to distinguish similarities and differences in pictures, colors, letters, numbers, words and sentences

15. Among the following methods for improving English-speaking ability in a bilingual class, the LEAST effective is to

    A. have pupils do oral reading from English basal readers
    B. present objects to the pupils for oral identification
    C. drill children on oral English patterns by having them make substitutions for words in the pattern
    D. use pictures as a basis for asking questions that require an oral response

16. The linguistic approach to reading is one frequently used in bilingual classes because of its emphasis on

    A. meaning in structural context
    B. interrelationships among all language arts skills
    C. sequentially graded reading skills
    D. phoneme-grapheme correspondence

17. All of the following are valid principles of second-language learning EXCEPT:

    A. Generalized rules should be developed for each structural pattern before extensive pattern drills on the structure
    B. Structural patterns should be presented only within a situation meaningful to the children in the group
    C. Meaningful written representations of a structural pattern should be related to oral production of the pattern
    D. A complete development of a topic should be accomplished before any new topic is presented

18. The pattern drill most suitable for practicing the changing of affirmative statements to interrogative statements would be

   A. repetition drill
   B. cued-response drill
   C. conversion drill
   D. expansion drill

19. All of the following areas enter into what is commonly termed "foreign accent" EXCEPT

   A. unidiomatic expressions
   B. incorrect stress patterns
   C. sound substitutions
   D. variations in speech melody

20. An INCORRECT instructional sequence of structural patterns would be to teach

   A. the interrogative pattern using inversion before the interrogative pattern using question words
   B. modifiers in relation to nouns before determiners in relation to nouns
   C. the affirmative statement pattern before the negative statement pattern
   D. present tense with the use of auxiliary verbs before simple past tense

21. In teaching children the melodic patterns of English, the bilingual teacher must emphasize that the "polite request" pattern in English requires:

   A. A generally rising intonation
   B. A generally falling intonation
   C. A rising intonation for each sound phrase, with a falling intonation in the final phrase
   D. A falling intonation for each sound phrase, with a rising intonation in the final phrase

22. To provide for the development of auditory discrimination in correcting the pronunciation of sounds, the bilingual teacher would most probably emphasize a drill of

   A. cued responses
   B. backwards build-up
   C. minimal pairs
   D. transformations

23. In planning for the use of class time, the bilingual teacher's first consideration should be

   A. needs, interests and abilities of the children
   B. curriculum bulletins for the grade
   C. grade-level textbooks
   D. plans followed by other teachers on the grade

24. In the audio-lingual approach of teaching English to non-native speakers, the children', s first contact with the language is through

   A. writing about their experiences
   B. practice and repetition of language patterns
   C. listening to oral language
   D. reading basal reader stories

25. The children in your bilingual class have been discussing a picture brought to class by one of the pupils. Of the following question, which would be most effective in promoting pupil thinking?

    A. What color dress is Jane wearing?
    B. Who came in the door as Jane left?
    C. Where did Jane place the book she was holding?
    D. Why do you think Jane looked worried?

KEY (CORRECT ANSWERS)

1.	D	11.	A
2.	A	12.	A
3.	A	13.	B
4.	C	14.	A
5.	D	15.	A
6.	A	16.	A
7.	D	17.	D
8.	B	18.	C
9.	C	19.	A
10.	A	20.	B

21. D
22. C
23. A
24. C
25. D

EXAMINATION SECTION
TEST 1

DIRECTIONS: Each question or incomplete statement is followed by several suggested answers or completions. Select the one the BEST answers the question or completes the statement. *PRINT THE LETTER OF THE CORRECT ANSWER IN THE SPACE AT THE RIGHT.*

1. Which of the following is NOT an example of an immediate constituent drill?

    A. Combining sentences or phrases in different ways
    B. Reducing clauses to phrases
    C. Adding expressions of time, place, or manner
    D. Changing sentence patterns from declarative to interrogative

    1.____

2. Which approach to second language teaching has received interest in recent years as an alternative to grammar-based approaches?

    A. Phonics
    B. Bilingual education
    C. Immersion
    D. Lexical approach

    2.____

3. Which of the following represents a pair of cognates?

    A. English *dog;* French *chien*
    B. English *pants;* German *hose*
    C. English *one;* Spanish *uno*
    D. English breakfast; French *petit déjeuner*

    3.____

4. Which of the following language teaching methods is descended from early methods of classical-language teaching?

    A. Reading
    B. Direct
    C. Audio-lingual
    D. Grammar-translation

    4.____

5. A teacher wants to investigate the usefulness and practicality of integrating computer-assisted language instruction into his classroom. The publication that would MOST likely be helpful to him is

    A. *Language Learning & Technology*
    B. *ADFL Bulletin*
    C. *ERIC/CLL Language Link*
    D. *Journal of Second Language Writing*

    5.____

6. When working with a structured conversation group, a language teacher should generally

    A. move from one student to the next in a circle
    B. steer the conversation when it strays from the assigned topic

    6.____

81

C. prevent students from interrupting until a student has finished speaking
D. step in to swing the conversation toward a student who has not been participating

7. Which of the following sentences is an example of the "regulatory" function of language? 7._____

   A. I'd like to know where you got these.
   B. Put it over there.
   C. I feel sad today.
   D. Suppose you were born a boy, rather than a girl.

8. Of the following organizations, which has a stated mission of improving the capacity of the United States to communicate in languages other than English, with an emphasis on strategic planning and public policy? 8._____

   A. National Foreign Language Center
   B. Center for Applied Linguistics
   C. Linguistic Society of America
   D. Modern Language Association

9. The purpose of an extensive reading program in the language classroom is usually to train the student to 9._____

   A. expand vocabulary and syntax in order to acquire a more sophisticated conversational style
   B. analyze and dissect ideas, in the target language, that are written in the target language
   C. write fluently in the target language for a readership of native speakers
   D. read directly and fluently in the target language for enjoyment, without the aid of a teacher

10. The first stage of most people's language acquisition can usually be described as 10._____

    A. holophrastic
    B. polymorphemic
    C. telegraphic
    D. derivational

11. In a news story describing a presidential press conference, the reporter describes the event as *a very convoluted answer to a very simple question.* In relation to the noun phrase *a very convoluted answer,* the press conference is the referent or 11._____

    A. inference
    B. intension
    C. sense
    D. extension

12. During the "recombination" stage of foreign-language writing instruction, a teacher should generally NOT 12._____

    A. have students expand sentences beyond their original syntactic boundaries
    B. permit students to check each other's in-class exercises

C. require students to make a recombination that involves a structural change and new vocabulary at the same point in the sentence
D. ask students to make novel recombinations around themes presented visually in class

13. Advantages to traditional reading-centered methods of foreign language instruction include each of the following, EXCEPT

    A. an opportunity for students to progress at their own rate
    B. higher probability of speech mastery
    C. heightened student interest in the people show speak the target language and their way of life
    D. students at different levels working with each other

14. In a small community with a large immigrant population from Cambodia, a teacher wants to research methods of teaching rudimentary Khmer to her American-born English-speaking students. Of the following, the most useful source of information on this topic would be the

    A. National Foreign Language Resource Center (NFLRC) at the University of Hawaii
    B. American Council on the Teaching of Foreign Languages
    C. Center for Advanced Language Research on Language Acquisition (CARLA)
    D. Center for Applied Linguistics

15. What is the term for the brief verbal responses used by a listener while another person is talking, such as *mm-hmm, okay, I see, yeah,* etc?

    A. Place markers
    B. Backchannels
    C. Crosstalk
    D. Conversational noise

16. Which of the following words is a polyseme?

    A. Demonstrate
    B. Mouth
    C. Stray
    D. Student

17. Which of the following is NOT typically an example of a grammatical morpheme?

    A. Noun
    B. Preposition
    C. Copula
    D. Verb inflection

18. Which of the following is an example of an integrative evaluation?

    A. A fill-in-the-blank test of students' knowledge of irregular plurals or tense forms
    B. The students' written arrangement of scrambled words and structural segments into meaningful compositions

C. A comprehension test in which students listen to a brief passage and then compose both oral and written answers to subsequent questions
D. An oral evaluation of students' production of certain sounds

19. Which of the following is ALWAYS an anaphor?

    A. Reflexive pronoun
    B. Agent
    C. Preposition
    D. Participle

20. During the 1980s, many language teachers began to reject the role of the traditional language laboratory in instruction. The primary reason for this was

    A. student distaste for the language laboratory setting
    B. the high costs associated with establishing and maintaining a laboratory
    C. the laboratory's integral relationship to audio-lingual methodologies
    D. insufficient supervision of student activities in the language laboratory setting

21. The word *striple* is a form that obeys the phonological rules for English, and yet it has no meaning. This word is an example of

    A. phonotactic
    B. logograph
    C. creative aspect
    D. lexical gap

22. During second-language acquisition, the strongest influence of the first language on the second is generally

    A. morphological
    B. phonological
    C. syntactic
    D. semantic

23. For most language teachers who are not native speakers of the target language, the biggest problem in modeling for students arises in the areas of

    A. semantics and syntax
    B. phonology and morphology
    C. articulation and pitch
    D. intonation and stress

24. Under ideal conditions, the most effective way of developing foreign language proficiency in the classroom is

    A. total immersion
    B. partial immersion
    C. the lexical approach
    D. the grammar-based approach

25. In acquiring a second language, learners appear to acquire morphemes in the same way that native speakers acquire them. This means that morphemes are acquired
    I. according to their morphological function
    II. according to their phonological form
    III. in a predictable sequence
    IV. at the same time

    A. I and III
    B. I and IV
    C. II and III
    D. II and IV

KEY (CORRECT ANSWERS)

1.	D	11.	D
2.	D	12.	C
3.	C	13.	B
4.	D	14.	A
5.	A	15.	B
6.	D	16.	B
7.	B	17.	A
8.	A	18.	C
9.	D	19.	A
10.	A	20.	C

21. D
22. B
23. D
24. A
25. A

TEST 2

DIRECTIONS: Each question or incomplete statement is followed by several suggested answers or completions. Select the one the BEST answers the question or completes the statement. *PRINT THE LETTER OF THE CORRECT ANSWER IN THE SPACE AT THE RIGHT.*

1. A student of Spanish says *Los aprende independencia* (It learns them independence), when what she really means is more accurately expressed as *Les ensena independencia* (It teaches them independence). The mistake the learner has made here could best be described as a(n)

    A. overgeneralization
    B. confusion of a pair of converses
    C. confusions of words with similar sound or spelling
    D. inappropriate use of synonyms

    1.____

2. In contemporary language studies, the _____ hypothesis can often be used to predict the amount of difficulty a student will have in learning certain elements of a second language.

    A. interlanguage
    B. markedness differential
    C. critical period
    D. contrastive analysis

    2.____

3. Misformation errors include each of the following types of errors, EXCEPT

    A. regularizations
    B. double markings
    C. alternating forms
    D. archiforms

    3.____

4. Which of the following publications generally offers the widest range of information to foreign language instructors on foreign language education, ESL, linguistics, and cross-cultural education?

    A. *ERIC/CLL Language Link*
    B. *PMLA Journal*
    C. *Language*
    D. *Language Learning & Technology*

    4.____

5. Disadvantages associated with the direct method of language instruction include each of the following, EXCEPT

    A. insufficient practice and repractice of structures in a coherent sequence
    B. a rigid and restrictive environment in which students can only learn what is prescribed by the teacher
    C. the unintended acquisition of "school pidgin"
    D. great demands on teachers' time and energy

    5.____

6. Which of the following student activities is an inductive approach to acquiring language structures?

    6.____

A. Students study rules, with examples, and practice exercises with the assistance of a computer.
B. Before the class session, students study a schematization of the structure, or a rule or paradigm.
C. The teacher demonstrates the new structure through activity in the classroom, using objects, pictures, actions, or sounds.
D. Students ask questions and construct some new examples of the rule in operation under the direction of the teacher.

7. The term "playing possum" is an example of a(n) 7._____

   A. idiom
   B. entailment
   C. dialect
   D. transitive

8. Language teachers who attempt to write short self-instructional programs for certain purposes should keep in mind that 8._____

   A. desired exit behaviors/outcomes should not be too specifically prescribed
   B. immediate confirmation of learning should be built into the program somehow
   C. emphasis should continually be placed on large exit goals, in order to give the learner something to look forward to
   D. optimal "step" size is usually larger than the inexperienced programmer realizes

9. The phrase *between you and I* is an example of 9._____

   A. structural hypercorrection
   B. implicature
   C. subcategorization restriction
   D. overgeneralization

10. Instruction in the lexical approach to foreign language instruction focuses on 10._____

    A. relatively fixed expressions that occur frequently in spoken language
    B. introducing a fixed number of certain parts of speech that are often used together in spoken language
    C. exceptions to the rules in conjugation, declension, plurals, and other "ending" variants
    D. traditional and tranformational grammar

11. The rules of syntax account for each of the following, EXCEPT 11._____

    A. structure-based paraphrases
    B. word meaning
    C. word order
    D. the grammaticality of sentences

12. A teacher wants to convey information to students about the cultural context of the target language. Which of the following organizations would be the BEST source for this kind of information? 12._____

    A. Center for Applied Linguistics
    B. National Foreign Language Center

C. American Council on the Teaching of Foreign Languages
D. Modern Language Association

13. Regardless of the program model for two-way immersion, it is generally recommended that the minority language be used for at least _____ percent of instructional time.

    A. 25
    B. 33
    C. 50
    D. 66

14. Research indicates that the "significance" of a spoken message to a listener begins with

    A. an interpretation of the speaker's intentions
    B. recognition vocabulary
    C. the situational context of the utterance
    D. a recognition of certain signal intonations

15. In its pure form, audio-lingual or "aural-oral" method of language instruction carries with it certain risks. Which of the following is NOT one of these?

    A. Students may become accomplished mimics, with little understanding of the structures they have learned to speak and write.
    B. Classroom routines can become tedious and fatiguing.
    C. Students are likely to neglect one type of skill—written or spoken over another as they are allowed to select their course of study.
    D. Students may develop troubles using practiced patterns to express their own meanings.

16. The word *himself* is an example of a(n)

    A. performative
    B. anaphor
    C. unbound
    D. tap

17. The sentence *The shepherd rounded up his sheeps* demonstrates an error in

    A. phonology
    B. morphology
    C. syntax
    D. semantics

18. The American Council on the Teaching of Foreign Languages' (ACTFL) Performance Guidelines for K-12 Learners
    I. describe the language proficiency of K-12 language learners in standards-based language programs
    II. describe language outcomes for students who begin instruction at different entry points
    III. are formulated in accordance with ACTFL Proficiency Guidelines and Standards for Foreign Languages
    IV. are organized according to domains and grade levels

A. I only
B. I, II and III
C. II and III
D. I, II, III and IV

19. The most effective forms of writing practice in a foreign language classroom are

    A. longer assignments that require research and investigation in the target language
    B. short, expressive, spontaneous assignments that are not supervised, but later discussed
    C. short, frequent assignments that are carefully corrected and discussed
    D. occasional summaries of material that has already been learned

20. Each of the following words is a "determiner," EXCEPT

    A. his
    B. an
    C. it
    D. this

21. When communication is the main learning objective in a language class, the proper role of reading should generally be to

    A. introduce and illuminate the culture of target-language speakers
    B. sharpen students' intellectual skills
    C. represent only variations of material that have been learned orally
    D. serve as a platform for launching spontaneous discussions

22. The Performance Assessment Initiative, designed to improve the ability of K-12 foreign language teachers to assess their students and integrate assessment practices with professional standards, includes each of the following activities, EXCEPT

    A. studying the advantages and drawbacks of computer-assisted instruction in the teaching of foreign language
    B. training in the administration and rating of the Student Oral Proficiency Assessment (SOPA)
    C. studying the advantages and drawbacks of distance learning technology in the teaching of foreign language
    D. maintaining an on-line foreign language assessment resource guide

23. A language teacher wants the instruction in her classroom to focus on content-area information; to engage students in activities that require critical thinking; and to provide opportunities for students to use the target language in meaningful contexts and complex ways. The most appropriate vehicle for this kind of learning is the

    A. analysis of discourse
    B. language laboratory
    C. thematic unit
    D. audio-lingual approach

24. In English, *gh* often serves to represent the [f] sound, and is therefore functioning as a(n)   24.____

    A. diphthong
    B. formant
    C. digraph
    D. argot

25. In the intermediate stages of target-language reading instruction, extensive reading   25.____
    materials can be made the basis for each of the following, EXCEPT

    A. oral reports to the rest of the class
    B. written compositions in which students deal with specific issues arising from the material
    C. detailed analytical discussion in the target language
    D. individual or group projects on some aspect of the culture presented by the material

---

KEY (CORRECT ANSWERS)

1.	B	11.	B
2.	B	12.	D
3.	B	13.	C
4.	A	14.	A
5.	B	15.	C
6.	C	16.	B
7.	A	17.	B
8.	B	18.	B
9.	A	19.	C
10.	A	20.	D

21. C
22. A
23. C
24. C
25. C

TEST 3

DIRECTIONS: Each question or incomplete statement is followed by several suggested answers or completions. Select the one the BEST answers the question or completes the statement. *PRINT THE LETTER OF THE CORRECT ANSWER IN THE SPACE AT THE RIGHT.*

1. The significant differences among two-way immersion models concern primarily the   1.____
    I. amount of time spent learning in English and in the minority language
    II. language in which initial literacy is provided
    III. size of the class being taught
    IV. cultural, linguistic and pedagogical assumptions

    A. I and II
    B. II, III and IV
    C. III and IV
    D. I, II, III and IV

2. Teachers who use the direct method of language instruction typically achieve the greatest success when students   2.____

    A. are given extensive reading practice, and are tested on comprehension
    B. begin with written forms and then move to speech
    C. can hear and practice the language outside the classroom
    D. apply an extensive vocabulary study as part of the classroom routine

3. Many Scandinavian languages form negatives by placing the negative after the main verb (i.e. *She ran not the race*). A Norwegian speaker learning English, however, may produce forms such as *She not ran the race,* even though such a construction never occurs in either English or the speaker's native language. Modern theories of second language acquisition would MOST likely attribute this form to   3.____

    A. negative transfer
    B. a temporally intermediate grammar that is different from both English and the speaker's native language
    C. the existence of a language universal of which the speaker is not aware, but nevertheless exists to form negatives in this way
    D. an error in contrastive analysis

4. In the earliest stages of foreign-language writing instruction, writing practice is best described as   4.____

    A. an experiment in structural variations
    B. free expression that occurs without comment or criticism
    C. strictly syntactic, at the word and phrase level
    D. an activity that consolidates work in other areas

5. A teacher wants to investigate different approaches for responding to brief foreign-language essays composed by her secondary students. Probably the most useful source of information for her would be the   5.____

    A. *Foreign Language Annals*
    B. *Journal of Second Language Writing*

C. ADFL Bulletin
D. *PMLA Journal*

6. The most significant role of task-based language laboratory activities is to

   A. provide a check for learners whose phonology is flawed
   B. limit the opportunities for learners fail in producing correct target-language speech
   C. provide learners with opportunities to use the target language contextually
   D. stimulate the learners' interest in the study of language

7. In the lexical approach to foreign language instruction, the phrase "by the way" would be categorized as a(n)

   A. institutionalized utterance
   B. polyword
   C. collocation
   D. word

8. Prior to a listening comprehension exercise, a language teacher can facilitate student success by activating prior knowledge. Which of the following is an effective way of doing this?

   A. Preparatory discussion
   B. Nonverbal cues
   C. Blackboard headlines or headings
   D. Topic focus

9. The word *young* is _____ of words such as *kitten, baby,* and *calf*.

   A. semantic property
   B. prosodic feature
   C. theme
   D. generalization

10. Because there is no English equivalent to the initial *ts-* sound to the Tswana word *tsetse,* the word is often pronounced as *teet-see* or *seet-see*. In this case, the developmental process involved in second language acquisition is

    A. consonant cluster simplification
    B. epenthesis
    C. devoicing
    D. metathesis

11. Which of the following sentences contains a factive verb?

    A. I see the man who stole my bicycle.
    B. I never knew my father.
    C. I realize you are bigger than I am.
    D. I used to be as short as she is.

12. Which of the following is NOT a guideline that should be used by teachers in designing and implementing an oral interview as an evaluative measure?

A. Examiners should work to make examinees forget they are in a testing situation
B. The pace of the interview should be set by the student
C. An objective measure such as a breakdown chart should be used to assess student performance
D. The interview should begin with role-playing or the study of a situational problem

13. An environment in which the focus of speakers is primarily on the content of the communication is labeled _____ language environment.

    A. formal
    B. natural
    C. foreign
    D. host

14. About a month into a beginning language class, a group of learners, after having demonstrated proficiency in the phonology of the target language, show signs of regression in pronunciation and intonation. Most likely, the reason for this is that

    A. the class has added several different activities to each session, leaving little time for sustained oral practice
    B. there has been a prolonged lag between oral introduction to the language and the graphic presentation of the material learned
    C. students have been speaking between and among themselves in the target language with too little teacher supervision
    D. the focus of classroom activity has now become the written exercise

15. The element of a second language that generally shows the strongest signs of being influenced by cultural knowledge is

    A. phonology
    B. morphology
    C. semantics
    D. syntax

16. Which of the following word pairs is the BEST example of a complementary pair?

    A. better; worse
    B. dumb; dumber
    C. wide; deep
    D. alive; dead

17. Which of the following contains an embedded sentence?

    A. She sees how things are.
    B. I know what you did last summer.
    C. I want to know how you know.
    D. I know that you did it.

18. Contemporary "block scheduling" models of instruction generally benefit language teachers in each of the following ways, EXCEPT

    A. fewer class interruptions
    B. greater frequency and depth of teacher/student interaction

C. fewer total students each semester
D. shorter preparation times

19. "Acoustic" phonetics address the distinctions in each of the following variables, EXCEPT

    A. duration of sounds
    B. loudness
    C. position of tongue and lips
    D. pitch

20. Which of the following is NOT a domain of performance specified by the American Council on the Teaching of Foreign Languages' (ACTFL) Performance Guidelines for K-12 Learners?

    A. Vocabulary Usage
    B. Cultural awareness
    C. Volubility
    D. Comprehensibility

21. Probably the LEAST appropriate students for the pure audio-lingual or "aural-oral" method of language instruction are

    A. students in a two-way immersion program
    B. young students with a facility for language learning
    C. younger children who enjoy mimicry and role-playing
    D. older, gifted students

22. A student of French writes: *Je sollicite une carriére à temps partiel an restaurant.* (I am applying for a part-time career at the restaurant). The use of the word *carriére* (career) in this sentence is most likely a(n)

    A. difficulty with idiom
    B. circumlocution
    C. inappropriate use of a synonym
    D. overgeneralization of superordinates

23. In the English language, the words *please* and *pleasant* reveal the likelihood of

    A. analogic change
    B. entailment
    C. internal reconstruction
    D. internal borrowing

24. Of the nine National Language Resource Centers in the United States, the one unique in its dedication to the professional development of K-12 foreign language teachers is located at

    A. University of Minnesota
    B. Iowa State University
    C. Michigan State University
    D. Georgetown University

25. A language teacher wants to create and manage a computer-delivered instructional module, but has no computer programming skills. The best resource for this teacher would be a(n)

    A. language lab system
    B. distance learning program
    C. existing Internet-based program
    D. commercially available authoring aid

25.____

KEY (CORRECT ANSWERS)

1.	A	11.	C
2.	C	12.	D
3.	B	13.	B
4.	D	14.	B
5.	B	15.	C
6.	C	16.	D
7.	B	17.	D
8.	A	18.	D
9.	A	19.	C
10.	A	20.	C

21. D
22. C
23. C
24. B
25. D

TEST 4

DIRECTIONS: Each question or incomplete statement is followed by several suggested answers or completions. Select the one the BEST answers the question or completes the statement. *PRINT THE LETTER OF THE CORRECT ANSWER IN THE SPACE AT THE RIGHT.*

1. In accordance with the American Council on the Teaching of Foreign Languages' (ACTFL) Performance Guidelines for K-12 Learners, a teacher specifies two learning goals for a student:

   demonstrate some accuracy in oral and written presentations when reproducing memorized words, phrases and sentences in the target language

   formulate oral and written presentations using a limited range of simple phrases and expressions based on familiar topics.

   The domain of performance being presented in these activities is

   A. presentational
   B. expressivity
   C. vocabulary usage
   D. language control

   1.____

2. The phrase *at the bottom of the staircase to the attic* is an example of

   A. recursion
   B. a spoonerism
   C. retroflex
   D. a transition network

   2.____

3. An English speaker who is learning Polish is puzzled by the long strings of consonants that sometimes appear in words—for example, the word *krzyzowka* (crossword). The English speaker consistently (and incorrectly) pronounces the beginning of this word *ker-ziz*. In making the word conform to a syllable structure acceptable in English, the speaker is transferring

   A. unstressed syllable deletion
   B. morphophonemic pronunciation
   C. an interlanguage form
   D. phonotactic constraints

   3.____

4. According to most communications research, the primary source of information for the listener of a spoken message is the

   A. intonation of the speaker
   B. sound quality of vowels and consonants
   C. rhythms of speech
   D. length of vowels

   4.____

5. The most common problem associated with natural language approaches to foreign language instruction is

   5.____

A. tedious, tiring classroom sessions that leave students unenthusiastic about learning another language
B. the lack of a "natural" environment in which students can learn languages
C. the tendency to emphasize the end product (written or spoken language) over the language learning process
D. an overbearing idealism that prevents consideration of practical applications

6. Which of the following learning objectives is MOST likely to take precedence in today's modern language classroom?

   A. Developing the students' intellectual abilities through the study of another language
   B. Providing students with the skills necessary for communicating orally, and to some degree in writing, in personal or career contexts, with the speakers of another language
   C. Increasing students' understanding of how language functions and to bring them to a greater awareness of the functioning of their native language
   D. Introducing a greater understanding of people across national barriers, by giving students insight into the ways of life and thinking of people who speak the target language

7. Activities of the Center for Applied Linguistics (CAL) include
   I. research
   II. design and development of instructional materials
   III. teacher education
   IV. program evaluation

   A. I and III
   B. II only
   C. II and IV
   D. I, II, III and IV

8. A language teacher designs an aural comprehension test to contain several different sections of discourse, with context supplied for each one. The teacher's reasons for choosing several selections, rather than a single extended one, probably do NOT include the idea that

   A. long-term retention is known to be triggered by sudden shifts in context
   B. a passage that is found to contain unanticipated difficulties for a significant number of students can be dropped from the final score/evaluation
   C. an initial error or misinterpretation will not ruin the whole test for the student
   D. the different sections are likely to tap several different semantic areas, making for a fairer assessment

9. Which of the following is NOT a benefit associated with the audio-lingual approach to language instruction?

   A. Rapidly acquired sense of achievement by students, who are able to use what they have learned
   B. Emphasis on innovation and invention with language forms
   C. Instruction offered in all types of language skills, both spoken and written
   D. Early competence and fluency within a limited range of content

10. Languages generally differ in whether or not they allow the omission of subject pronouns in tensed clauses-for example, Spanish drops the pronoun el (he) in the sentence *Está enfermo,* while English requires that the sentence be written with an overt subject, as *He is sick.* According to modern language theory, this difference signifies a variation in the _____ universals of language.

    A. statistical
    B. absolute
    C. implicational
    D. parametric

11. Generally, two-way bilingual immersion programs strive to promote each of the following, EXCEPT

    A. grade-level academic achievement
    B. bilingualism and biliteracy
    C. positive cross-cultural attitudes and behaviors
    D. simultaneous interchange between first and second languages

12. A "conversation course" in a foreign language is best evaluated by

    A. a lengthy oral interview for each student, supplemented by a listening comprehension test
    B. small-group dialogues, supplemented by aural discrimination tests
    C. tests in all skill areas: listening, speaking, reading, and writing
    D. a report on a personal research project, followed by an oral question-and-answer period

13. The server-based setup for many contemporary language laboratories typically enables each of the following, EXCEPT

    A. teachers' incorporation of networked lab resources into regular classroom instruction
    B. dedicated videodisc players or other peripherals for every computer workstation
    C. teachers and learners in remote locations can use instructional materials
    D. simultaneous access of video or audio resources by multiple users

14. The sentence *Why you give him your bicycle?* is an example of an error in

    A. syntax
    B. morphology
    C. semantics
    D. phonology

15. A student's first expressive composition assignments in a foreign language will be LEAST likely to ask the student to

    A. describe
    B. investigate
    C. summarize
    D. explain

16. A teacher wants to investigate the nature of multilingualism and multiculturalism as they apply to classroom instruction. Of the following, the most useful source of information would probably be the

    A. National Foreign Language Center
    B. Center for Applied Linguistics
    C. Center for Advanced Language Research on Language Acquisition (CARLA)
    D. Modern Language Association

17. Typically, evaluations that ask a student to translate a reading passage from the foreign language into the native language are valid tests of each of the following, EXCEPT

    A. knowledge of stylistic differences and cultural contrasts between the foreign and native languages
    B. literal and figurative comprehension of the foreign language
    C. the expression of nuance and idiom in the native language
    D. felicity of expression in the foreign language

18. A student speaks the following sentence: *Mary loved Tina and she loved Bart.* In vocally emphasizing the pronoun *she*, the student is making it clear that Tina, not Mary, loved Bart. This is an example of

    A. contrastive stress
    B. referent marking
    C. derivation
    D. iconicity

19. To study the effects of classroom activities on students' language production, a teacher designs a study in which he or another observer simply records the events of several class periods, which are later interpreted by the teacher. The mode of research being used by the teacher is

    A. psychometric study
    B. discourse analysis
    C. interaction analysis
    D. ethnographic analysis

20. Which of the following is a non-count noun?

    A. Boy
    B. School
    C. Water
    D. Airplane

21. In designing a unit test, a teacher faces the challenge of making sure she measures all the varied components of target language competence and skill that were learned in the unit. The teacher faces the problem of

    A. efficiency
    B. validity
    C. generalizability
    D. scope

22. The statement "He suggested her to go" is an example of

    A. archiform
    B. misformation
    C. alternating forms
    D. double marking

23. Students in a classroom read material they have been using orally, but the material includes recombinations and variations. This stage of reading instruction is generally known as

    A. familiarization
    B. intension
    C. autonomy
    D. expansion

24. In English, the plural of the noun *cow* is known to have changed from its earlier form, *kine*, to *cows*, in a generalization of the plural formation rule. This is an example of

    A. analogic change
    B. time deixis
    C. convention
    D. entailment

25. Probably the LEAST useful or valid type of foreign language reading comprehension test is one in which the student

    A. writes a translation of a passage into to the native language
    B. answers foreign language questions in the native language
    C. answers foreign language questions in the foreign language
    D. selects correct answers from multiple-choice items in the foreign language

KEY (CORRECT ANSWERS)

1. D
2. A
3. D
4. B
5. D

6. B
7. D
8. A
9. B
10. D

11. D
12. A
13. B
14. A
15. B

16. C
17. D
18. A
19. D
20. C

21. D
22. A
23. A
24. A
25. C

EXAMINATION SECTION
TEST 1

DIRECTIONS: Each question or incomplete statement is followed by several suggested answers or completions. Select the one the BEST answers the question or completes the statement. *PRINT THE LETTER OF THE CORRECT ANSWER IN THE SPACE AT THE RIGHT.*

1. In the target language, a student is able to participate in simple, direct conversations on generally predictable topics related to daily activities and her personal environment. She is also able to obtain and give information by asking and answering questions. According to the American Council on the Teaching of Foreign Languages' (ACTFL) Proficiency Guidelines, this student would, at the very least, be classified as

    A. novice
    B. intermediate
    C. advanced
    D. superior

    1.____

2. Which of the following traits is most predictive of second-language acquisition?

    A. Extroversion
    B. Field dependence
    C. Advanced age
    D. Instrumental motivation

    2.____

3. In class, a student says *Me ramo Lloberto* instead of *Me llamo Roberto* (My name is Robert). The student has done what is known as

    A. gliding
    B. epenthesis
    C. metathesis
    D. structural hypercorrection

    3.____

4. Which of the following qualities would generally be MOST desirable in a grammar exercises found in a traditional textbook?

    A. A mixture of target-language and native-language forms within exercises
    B. A limited range of vocabulary used within one set of exercises
    C. Simultaneous manipulation of several grammatical features in complicated interrelationships
    D. Rapid progress from one aspect of a grammatical feature to another

    4.____

5. Which of the following is NOT a classroom activity that will help preadolescent students to learn the phonology of a target language?

    A. Direct instruction in the phonological differences between native and target languages
    B. Activities, such as mimicry and role-playing, which are largely repetitive
    C. Participation in games and competitions
    D. Composing and singing songs in the target language

    5.____

6. Which of the following speech sounds is typically classified as a "liquid?"

    6.____

A. *s* in *Saturday*
B. *r* in *runner*
C. *y* in *yesterday*
D. *d* in *difference*

7. A learner of French says *J'ai lepetit argent* (I have small money) to mean *J'alpeu d'argent* (I have little money). The learner's statement is most likely a case of

    A. difficulty with idiom
    B. the use of a converse
    C. circumlocution
    D. overgeneralization

8. Which of the following is an example of back-to-back phonemes?

    A. Who's that?
    B. He's sweating.
    C. You couldn't not recognize him.
    D. I never knew him.

9. For most language teachers, the central problem of teaching to promote spontaneous expression in another language is knowing

    A. the linguistic resources they will need to communicate
    B. what students with minimum requirements will know and be able to do in particular situations
    C. the contexts in which learners will want or need to express themselves
    D. what communicative functions language learners will need to fulfill at the threshold level

10. The sentence *I saw a man with binoculars* is an example of

    A. structural ambiguity
    B. retroflex
    C. semantic substitution
    D. misformation

11. In the early stages of second-language reading instruction, especially in activities involving recombination conversations or dialogues, it is important for the teacher to avoid the students' engaging in

    A. thinking and reading in word groups, rather than complete sentences
    B. word-for-word translation of a reading passage
    C. taking an initial "once-over" glance at the passage before reading
    D. "backward-buildup" techniques for constructing language segments

12. The underlying claim of those who practice the lexical approach to foreign language instruction is that language production

    A. is a syntactic rule-governed process
    B. must begin with words
    C. is the retrieval of large phrasal units from memory
    D. occurs simultaneously on incoming and outgoing paths of communication

13. In second-language acquisition, the purpose of _____ is to identify irregularities in interlanguage forms.

    A. developmental processes
    B. structural hypercorrection
    C. error analysis
    D. semantic substitution

14. Newer block scheduling models in schools typically involve each of the following implications for language teachers, EXCEPT the

    A. likelihood of more fast-paced coverage
    B. emphasis on grammar and structural practice over communicative skills
    C. rigor of organizing principles, both for units and lessons
    D. need for more and varied classroom activities

15. Elicitation tasks that focus learners' attention on the form of the language they produce, rather than on meaning, are known as _____ tasks.

    A. taxonomic
    B. strategic
    C. linguistic manipulation
    D. natural communication

16. Which of the following statements about the audio-lingual approach to language instruction is FALSE?

    A. In early instructional stages, students are introduced to an extensive vocabulary.
    B. When writing instruction begins, it is usually imitative in nature.
    C. At the first level of instruction, learning is often based on dialogues containing commonly used expressions and structures.
    D. After basic spoken forms are learned, pattern drills often become the main classroom activity.

17. Each of the following is a guideline that should be used by language teachers during the "recombination dictation" phase of writing instruction, EXCEPT

    A. the teacher should dictate recombinations at a normal rate of utterance, without slowing or distortion
    B. students should be encouraged to repeat aloud what has been dictated before writing it
    C. each phrase should be repeated clearly once before students are expected to write it
    D. recombinations written from dictation should contain elements that are distinctly different from what the students have already learned

18. Which of the following publications focuses on the field of theoretical linguistics?

    A. *Language*
    B. *ERIC/CLL Language Link*
    C. *Journal of Second Language Writing*
    D. *PMLA Journal*

19. A task-based language laboratory activity generally does NOT

    A. have a goal or purpose that requires the use of the target language.
    B. draw the student's attention to specific structures within the target language itself
    C. involve the student in a way that intrinsically motivates him/her and creates a desire to excel
    D. create a learning environment that cannot be recreated in the regular classroom

    19.____

20. In the phrase *a very old man with enormous wings,* the "head" of the phrase is the word

    A. a
    B. with
    C. old
    D. man

    20.____

21. Which of the following classroom activities demonstrates that a teacher is using the direct method of language instruction?

    A. Target-language texts are read aloud by the teacher and students, and the students are encouraged to seek comprehension by inferring meanings of unknown elements from the context.
    B. Students translate consecutive prose passages from the native to the target language, and vice-versa.
    C. Students read extended passages (several pages) in the target language, and then their comprehension is tested by questions on the content of the reading material, rather than by translation.
    D. Students learn dialogue sentence by memorization, one by one, by continually repeating a recorded sentence until they are repeating it accurately and fluently.

    21.____

22. Generally, studies of the Student Oral Proficiency Assessment (SOPA) reveal that it

    A. is not an accurate measure of the proficiency of immersion students
    B. has been adequately validated for use in the instruction of some languages, but not others
    C. is most discriminating when administered to students who have completed at least two years of foreign language study
    D. would best be described as a teacher observation matrix, rather than an assessment

    22.____

23. Traditionally, many foreign language teachers have presented cultural material to students through exposition and explanation—discussing at length, or presenting in films or slides, the geographic, historical, artistic, scientific, and institutional aspects of the society of the target language. Common objections to this method of introducing a foreign culture in the language classroom include the idea that it

    I. detracts from the fundamental task of language learning and communication
    II. reinforces existing stereotypes about the society of the target language
    III. is more appropriate for other subject areas in the school
    IV. consists of the absorption of a number of uninterpreted and unrelated facts

    A. I and II
    B. I, II and III
    C. I, III and IV
    D. I, II, III and IV

    23.____

24. The Spanish tilde (~), the French cedilla (C), and the German umlaut (") are all examples   24.____
    of
    A. diphthongs
    B. diacritics
    C. entailments
    D. phonotactics

25. Language teachers generally believe that the most effective student exercises in foreign-   25.____
    language listening
    A. do not allow the listener to "back up" and hear a message a second time
    B. require the listener to act in some way as a result of what he/she has heard
    C. focus on the most recently learned structures and vocabulary
    D. introduce new vocabulary which the listener must define through context

KEY (CORRECT ANSWERS)

1.	B	11.	B
2.	A	12.	C
3.	C	13.	C
4.	B	14.	B
5.	A	15.	C
6.	B	16.	A
7.	D	17.	D
8.	B	18.	A
9.	C	19.	B
10.	A	20.	D

21. A
22. C
23. C
24. B
25. B

TEST 2

DIRECTIONS: Each question or incomplete statement is followed by several suggested answers or completions. Select the one the BEST answers the question or completes the statement. *PRINT THE LETTER OF THE CORRECT ANSWER IN THE SPACE AT THE RIGHT.*

1. The official publication of the American Council on the Teaching of Foreign Languages (ACTFL) is

    A. *Journal of Second Language Writing*
    B. *Foreign Language Annals*
    C. *Language Learning & Technology*
    D. *Language*

    1.____

2. The various "oral" and "natural" teaching methods, which advocate the learning of a language through the association of words and phrases with objects and actions, without the use of the native language by teachers or students, are collectively known as the _____ method of language teaching.

    A. direct
    B. grammar-translation
    C. reading
    D. audio-lingual

    2.____

3. Which of the following is a term used to refer to the speech or writing of foreign language learners in the foreign language?

    A. Uberlanguage
    B. Instrumental language
    C. Interlanguage
    D. Positive transfer

    3.____

4. A native Spanish speaker, accustomed to the pronoun drop in sentences such as *No veo* (I don't see), consistently uses the same pattern in English - for example, saying *Don't see* instead of *I don't see.* This is an example of

    A. negative transfer
    B. interlanguage
    C. positive transfer
    D. a markedness differential

    4.____

5. Of the following, probably the most important factor in whether a foreign-language message will be understood by a listener is the

    A. length of pauses and language segments
    B. intonation of the speaker
    C. rate of delivery
    D. amount of repetition in the message

    5.____

6. Which of the following student activities is a deductive approach to acquiring language structures?

    6.____

108

A. Students study a rule or paradigm, and then look at examples of its use.
B. Students listen to examples of the structure in use and then perform guided exercises that involve use of the structure.
C. The teacher distributes several example sentences that contain the structure, and then students discuss the commonalities of structures they observe in the sentence.
D. In a reading passage, students encounter a new language structure in a meaningful context.

7. In the lexical approach to foreign language instruction, the phrase "community service" would be categorized as a(n)

   A. polyword
   B. word
   C. collocation
   D. institutionalized utterance

8. In most modern Indo-European languages, intonation becomes MOST important when student speakers attempt to

   A. form lists
   B. suggest alternatives
   C. ask questions
   D. change the case of pronouns

9. Generally, writing weaknesses in advanced language classes can be attributed to

   A. poor pronunciation and intonation carried over from lessons in phonology
   B. insufficient vocabulary
   C. writing weaknesses in the native language
   D. a lack of systematic practice in earlier stages of the language course

10. Which of the following represents the clearest parent/daughter language relationship?

    A. English-German
    B. Greek-Sanskrit
    C. Latin-French
    D. Latin-English

11. In the middle of an extensive reading program, it becomes clear to a teacher that students are not conscious at all times of the exact meaning of every item in each sentence. The teacher should

    A. collect data on which items or structures are not being understood, and supplement reading exercises with pattern drills
    B. know that such close attention to detail isn't necessarily a feature of native-language reading, either
    C. look for reading materials with more repetitive structures
    D. spot-test students' understanding periodically with short translation exercises

12. Which of the following is NOT a type of addition error?

    A. Double marking
    B. Regularization

C. Misformation
D. Simple addition

13. A student of Spanish translates *Si compro una casa tengo en cuenta el precio y la localización* as *If I buy a house I have in account the price and the location*. More accurately, the last part of the sentence would translate as *I consider the price and the location*. In translating *tengo en cuenta* literally as *I have in account*, the student has demonstrated a(n)

    A. difficulty with an idiomatic verb
    B. confusion of a pair of converses
    C. immature interlanguage
    D. confusion of words with similar sound

14. To study the effect of classroom activities on students' language production, a teacher designs an experiment in which students are divided into control and experimental groups, and writes pre-tests and post-tests for both. The mode of research being used by the teacher is

    A. ethnographic analysis
    B. discourse analysis
    C. psychometric study
    D. interaction analysis

15. Which of the following word pairs is the BEST example of a gradable pair?

    A. hungry; thirsty
    B. birth; death
    C. height; weight
    D. warm; cool

16. Which of the following is generally NOT a guideline for the use of pattern drills in a foreign language classroom?

    A. Drills should be recited with a visual support for the script.
    B. A pattern should be considered "learned" when students can use it in conversational exchanges.
    C. Students should hear a pattern several times before being asked to repeat it.
    D. After the initial phase, students should produce variants of the pattern with some differences in lexical content.

17. The distinction between task-based language laboratory activities and programmed instruction is that one focuses on _____; the other on _____.

    A. listening comprehension/questioning skills
    B. reading, writing and orthography/speech and phonology
    C. exceptions to rules and paradigms/strict adherence
    D. communicative fluency/ linguistic accuracy

18. In accordance with the American Council on the Teaching of Foreign Languages' (ACTFL) Performance Guidelines for K-12 Learners, a teacher specifies two learning goals for a student:

    •express one's own thoughts using sentences and strings of sentences when interacting on familiar topics in present time

    •use pronunciation and intonation patterns that can be understood by a native speaker accustomed to interacting with language learners

    The communication mode being covered by these activities is

    A. interpretive
    B. presentational
    C. comprehensive
    D. interpersonal

19. The most significant problem associated with attempts at norm-referenced evaluations in most language classrooms is that

    A. students do not know in advance what knowledge they will be required to demonstrate
    B. the teacher usually does not have the numbers to expect a normal distribution among the students
    C. norms are unfixed, constantly evolving standards for evaluation
    D. they invalidate the entire concept of mastery learning

20. In the sentence *Jasper dug a trench with his shovel,* the "instrument" is represented by the word

    A. Jasper
    B. shovel
    C. trench
    D. dug

21. Which of the following is NOT a typical way in which a teacher using the direct method of language instruction might modify it in order to counteract inaccuracy and vagueness?

    A. Brief last resort definitions or explanations in the native language
    B. More practice in grammatical structures, sometimes with the use of substitution tables
    C. Addition of functional grammatical explanations in the native language
    D. Use of extended translation assignments

22. Which of the following are converse antonyms?

    A. *Dead* and *alive*
    B. *Employer* and *employee*
    C. *Man* and *girl*
    D. *Hot* and *cold*

23. As part of his professional development, a foreign language teacher wants to attend a seminar that will provide training in theoretical linguistics. He should contact the

    A. Modern Language Association
    B. Center for Advanced Language Research on Language Acquisition (CARLA)
    C. Linguistic Society of America
    D. Center for Applied Linguistics

24. A learner of English consistently misarranges the auxiliaries in interrogative sentences to conform to the pattern of his first language (i.e., *What I am supposed to do?*). This is an example of

    A. positive transfer
    B. an interlanguage form
    C. negative transfer
    D. markedness differential

25. A student who pronounces the name Lillian as "Wiwian" is

    A. gliding
    B. telegraphing
    C. lisping
    D. sonorizing

KEY (CORRECT ANSWERS)

1. B
2. A
3. C
4. A
5. A

6. A
7. C
8. C
9. D
10. C

11. B
12. C
13. A
14. C
15. D

16. A
17. D
18. D
19. B
20. B

21. D
22. B
23. C
24. C
25. A

TEST 3

DIRECTIONS: Each question or incomplete statement is followed by several suggested answers or completions. Select the one the BEST answers the question or completes the statement. *PRINT THE LETTER OF THE CORRECT ANSWER IN THE SPACE AT THE RIGHT.*

1. The only word-final obstruent allowed in the Portuguese language is 5. When a Portuguese student is introduced to the word *dog*, she consistently pronounces it as *dog-i*, placing an *i* in the word-final position. The student is

   A. illustrating a projection problem
   B. creating an English gloss
   C. reflecting a developmental process typical of first-language learners
   D. transferring a phonotactic constraint from her first language

2. A teacher devises an evaluation that consists of a foreign language passage in which every fifth word is missing. Students are expected to read the test carefully and then fill in all omitted words according to their projections of the evolving meaning. This is an example of a(n)

   A. decision tree
   B. discrete-point test
   C. cloze test
   D. tagmemic

3. The use of the word "eated" as a past tense for "to eat" is an example of

   A. archiform
   B. ambiguous error
   C. interlingual error
   D. regularization

4. The Foreign Language Test Database, a searchable database of secondary and college level tests in languages other than English, is maintained by the

   A. Center for Applied Linguistics
   B. American Council on the Teaching of Foreign Languages
   C. Modern Language Association
   D. National Capital Language Resource Center

5. The communicative approach to language teaching is MOST likely to rely on

   A. programmed instruction
   B. intensive reading
   C. real-life simulations
   D. traditional language laboratory settings

6. Which of the following activities would NOT typically be used to develop a student's knowledge of a language's lexical chains?

   A. Guessing the meaning of vocabulary items from context
   B. Word-for-word first and second language comparisons and translations

C. Noting and recording language patterns
D. Intensive reading and listening in the target language

7. Many second language learners face what is known as the "projection problem" they must acquire grammatical knowledge that cannot be inferred solely from the data they are exposed to in the course of their studies. In modern language theory, the explanation for this ability lies in the existence of

   A. markedness differentials
   B. interlanguage
   C. developmental processes
   D. language universals

7._____

8. Which of the following is NOT a disadvantage associated with the grammar-translation method of language teaching?

   A. Academic and out-of-context forms of language used in instruction
   B. Unnecessarily detailed vocabulary
   C. Little demand on students' intellectual skills
   D. Largely passive student role

8._____

9. Which of the following is NOT one of the nine National Language Resource Centers established by the U. S. Department of Education?

   A. Center for Advanced Language Research on Language Acquisition (CARLA) at the University of Minnesota
   B. Ohio State University Foreign Language Center
   C. Center for Language Education and Research (CLEAR) at Michigan State University
   D. National Foreign Language Center (NFLC) at the University of Maryland

9._____

10. Students in a foreign language classroom spend some time each day practicing the construction of several sentences of very different meanings, while retaining the same basic structural pattern. These types of exercises are known as

    A. constituents
    B. morphemics
    C. tagmemics
    D. conversions

10._____

11. In the sentence *Joseph is the programmer,* the verb *is* can be considered an example of a(n)

    A. bound morpheme
    B. copula
    C. coreferent
    D. reflexive

11._____

12. In the study of language, the one area in which adult learners tend to lag behind younger learners is

    A. phonology
    B. morphology

12._____

C. syntax
D. semantics

13. Even in contemporary classrooms, some language teachers place an overriding emphasis on reading competence in the target language. The research finding that is most directly responsible for this is that

    A. the majority of American students study a foreign language for only two years
    B. the motivation for most foreign language students is instrumental, rather than integrative
    C. most students' real-world experiences with the target language will be in written rather than spoken form
    D. there was not enough emphasis on reading skills in the core curriculum of most schools that offered foreign language instruction

14. Which of the following illustrates that an acoustic difference in a learner's pronunciation of a word has become a phonemic difference?

    A. The *a* in *able* is pronounced like the *e* in *tent*
    B. The *t* in *butter* is pronounced like the *d* in *shudder*
    C. The *v* in *every* is pronounced as an *f*
    D. The *o* in *dog* is pronounced like the *u* in *luck*

15. The FIRST stage of foreign-language writing instruction is generally a period of

    A. recombination
    B. aural-written reproduction
    C. notation
    D. expressive writing

16. Which of the following is a glide?

    A. a in *aviary*
    B. w in *we*
    C. f in *field*
    D. ch in *chair*

17. In the target language, a student is able to respond to simple questions on everyday aspects of life. He is also able to convey minimal meaning to native speakers experienced in communicating with language learners, by using isolated words, lists, and memorized phrases. According to the American Council on the Teaching of Foreign Languages' (ACTFL) Proficiency Guidelines, this student would, at the very least, be classified as

    A. novice
    B. intermediate
    C. advanced
    D. superior

18. The word face has several closely related but slightly different meanings (the face of a person, the face of a clock, the face of a building, etc.). Which of the following terms is used to describe such a word?

A. Polymorphemic
B. Recursive
C. Polysemous
D. Binary valued

19. Compared to a conversation-facilitation dialogue, a grammar-demonstration dialogue typically

   A. use several different examples of the grammatical structure to be studied
   B. have longer, more involved sentences
   C. provide less context from which students will generalize about rules, operation, or function
   D. are more likely to be memorized by students

20. Which of the following pairs of words have semantic overlap?

   A. *Hot* and *fluid*
   B. *Cloud* and *lake*
   C. *Bridge* and *steam*
   D. *Monk* and *nephew*

21. Which of the following sentences is an example of the "heuristic" function of language?

   A. There are ten children in that family.
   B. If I were younger, my knees wouldn't hurt me so much.
   C. Where does he live?
   D. Have a nice day.

22. The words *canine* and *pooch* have different

   A. anaphors
   B. connotations
   C. idiolects
   D. denotations

23. Reading aloud in a beginning or intermediate language classroom is probably BEST described as an activity that

   A. tests pronunciation and comprehension almost simultaneously
   B. can help individual students, working by themselves after initial practice in sound-symbol correspondence, to extract meaning from graphic material
   C. should be a test of pronunciation only after a passage has been read silently for comprehension
   D. often stimulates further cultural interest from young learners of a language

24. What is the term for a bound morpheme attached to the stem or root morpheme?

   A. Affix
   B. Retroflex
   C. Continuant
   D. Extension

25. Probably the best way for a teacher to gain insight into the effect of specific tasks on students' language production-and, over time, their language development-is to 25.____
   A. record, transcribe, and analyze the students' discourse in the target language
   B. observe, record, and analyze the students' responses in a language lab setting
   C. test students in all areas of language skill-listening, reading, writing, and speaking
   D. assign frequent writing practice and discuss assignments immediately upon completion

---

KEY (CORRECT ANSWERS)

1.	D	11.	B
2.	C	12.	A
3.	D	13.	A
4.	D	14.	D
5.	C	15.	C
6.	B	16.	B
7.	D	17.	A
8.	C	18.	C
9.	D	19.	B
10.	C	20.	D

21. C
22. B
23. C
24. A
25. A

TEST 4

DIRECTIONS: Each question or incomplete statement is followed by several suggested answers or completions. Select the one the BEST answers the question or completes the statement. *PRINT THE LETTER OF THE CORRECT ANSWER IN THE SPACE AT THE RIGHT.*

1. Foreign language teachers who choose the "activist" model over a more "formalist" approach generally

    A. spend much time on language analysis
    B. rely on written forms of the language, rather than speech
    C. prefer an inductive apprehension of language forms
    D. supply students with information and ask them to apply it

    1._____

2. Which of the following classroom activities will help students to avoid phonemic enunciation errors?

    A. Delayed oral practice
    B. Aural discrimination drills
    C. Dramatization
    D. Structural pattern drills

    2._____

3. A teacher seeks innovative and successful methods of foreign language instruction. The publication most likely to present and discuss a wide range of these methods is

    A. *Language*
    B. PMLA Journal
    C. *Foreign Language Annals*
    D. *ADFL Bulletin*

    3._____

4. A teacher plays for students an audiotape of a target-language conversation between two people in a public place. After the conversation has been played twice, the teacher asks several questions (i.e., Who was talking? Where were they when you started listening in? What were they talking about?) that will be answered in the target language. This type of exercise is most likely to be used by a teacher using the _____ approach to language teaching

    A. grammar-translation
    B. audio-lingual
    C. discriminatory
    D. communicative

    4._____

5. A good structural pattern drill should

    A. make several lexical changes between one cue-response item and the next
    B. drill students consistently through a series of twelve to fifteen cue-response items
    C. be purely imitative
    D. focus on structural features that have been encountered already by the students

    5._____

6. In the addition of the suffix *-ish* to *girl*, forming the word *girlish*, the suffix is an example of a(n)

    6._____

A. derivational morpheme
B. velar
C. geminate
D. circumfix R

7. A student of German writes: *Letztes Jahr, stopple meine Mutter zu leben von einer verldngerten Krankheit ihres Inneren und Lungen.* The sentence translates literally as *Last year, my mother stopped living from a prolonged illness of her heart and lungs.* The student has demonstrated a(n)

    A. inappropriate use of a synonym
    B. overgeneralization
    C. difficulty with idiom
    D. circumlocution

8. The statement "I hardly never go" is an example of

    A. double marking
    B. omission
    C. archiform
    D. developmental error

9. Which of the following is NOT a prosodic element of language?

    A. Articulation
    B. Internal juncture
    C. Stress
    D. Syllabification

10. When a student performs a point-by-point comparison of the grammars of two languages, he or she is conducting a(n)

    A. contrastive analysis
    B. phoneticization
    C. transformational analysis
    D. node parsing

11. Elicitation tasks that focus learners' attention on the idea or opinion being expressed, rather than on the language forms used, are known as _____ tasks.

    A. code alternation
    B. creative construction
    C. linguistic manipulation
    D. natural communication

12. In the phrase *into the inky, bubbling mud pot,* the "head" of the phrase is the word

    A. pot
    B. mud
    C. the
    D. into

13. Which of the following phrases or sentences would be classified as an "institutionalized utterance" by the lexical approach to foreign language instruction?

A. upside down
B. collateral damage
C. It's as easy as ...
D. May I get you anything?

14. Which of the following sentences is an example of the "instrumental" function of language?

    A. If it were possible to go back in time, I would make sure this had never happened.
    B. It makes me angry when you act like this.
    C. How did these get here?
    D. Could you tell me where I might find a taxicab?

15. A student explains to his foreign language instructor that she wants to learn a second language in order to get a job in international banking. The student's motivation for learning a second language is described as

    A. locutionary
    B. instrumental
    C. operational
    D. integrative

16. In most beginning foreign language classrooms, it is advisable for the teacher to convey cultural concepts related to the target language

    A. with an emphasis on the exotic and outlandish
    B. in a much-simplified framework that is easily understandable to early level students
    C. dispassionately and objectively
    D. in a primarily historical context

17. In accordance with the American Council on the Teaching of Foreign Languages' (ACTFL) Performance Guidelines for K-12 Learners, a teacher specifies two learning goals for a student:

    •understand main ideas and significant details on a variety of topics found in products of a target culture, such as those presented on television, radio, video, or live presentations

    • develop one's awareness of tone, style, and author perspective

    The communication mode being covered by these activities is

    A. cultural
    B. interpretive
    C. presentational
    D. interpersonal

18. In audio-lingual or "aural-oral" approach to language learning, the first language skills taught are associated with

    A. speaking
    B. writing

C. listening
D. reading

19. The simple word *house* is often used in English to express the complex French concept embodied in the word *maison*. This is an example of the use of a(n)   19.____

    A. figurehead
    B. holophrast
    C. gloss
    D. theta-criterion

20. Target-language reading materials for an extensive reading program should generally meet each of the following requirements, EXCEPT that   20.____

    A. the style should involve a certain degree of repetition
    B. stories and articles should be divided into brief sections
    C. novelties of vocabulary should not coincide with structural difficulties
    D. backgrounders should stress the exotic and unfamiliar

21. A teacher wants to present a brief unit comparing the literary works of America and the countries where foreign language of the classroom is spoken. Probably the best source for this kind of information would be the   21.____

    A. American Council on the Teaching of Foreign Languages
    B. Modern Language Association
    C. Center for Applied Linguistics
    D. National Capital Language Resource Center

22. Probably the most significant issue faced by language teachers as they encounter contemporary block scheduling models involves   22.____

    A. continuity from level to level
    B. timing of standardized tests
    C. frequency of one-on-one interaction with students
    D. appropriateness of course content and methodology

23. The idea that language-acquisition abilities atrophy with age is known as the _____ hypothesis.   23.____

    A. markedness differential
    B. interlanguage
    C. critical period
    D. contrastive analysis

24. Which of the following is NOT typically an activity involved in the "reproduction" stage of foreign-language writing instruction?   24.____

    A. Writing sentences that are read aloud and repeated by the teacher
    B. Reproducing practiced sentences with adaptations
    C. Writing a learned phrase in response to a question, or as a description of a visual aid
    D. Rewriting sentences without reference to a printed version

25. A learner of Spanish, relying on experience with Spanish morphemes, misinterprets the meaning of the word *estulto* (stupid) as "out of stupidity." This is an example of

    A. creating a gloss
    B. phonotactic constraint
    C. deceptive transparency
    D. contrastive analysis

25. _____

KEY (CORRECT ANSWERS)

1.	C	11.	D
2.	B	12.	D
3.	C	13.	D
4.	D	14.	D
5.	D	15.	B
6.	A	16.	C
7.	D	17.	B
8.	A	18.	C
9.	A	19.	C
10.	A	20.	D

21.	B
22.	A
23.	C
24.	B
25.	C

www.ingramcontent.com/pod-product-compliance
Lightning Source LLC
Chambersburg PA
CBHW081826300426
44116CB00014B/2499